THE REAL
ABOLITIONISTS

Other books by Michael Nathan-Pepple:

1. ALL ABOUT ANTIGUA AND BARBUDA
A travel guide that describes the history and heritage of the twin island nation of Antigua and Barbuda, and highlights some of its most popular sites and attractions.

2. HISTORICAL CHURCHES OF
THE CARIBBEAN ISLAND OF ANTIGUA
The book explores the complex relationship between the Older Established Churches, Slavery and the conversion of enslaved Africans to Christianity. It also includes beautiful photographs and history of each historical church featured in the book.

3. AMAZING AFRICA
The book seeks to change the narrative by telling the African story. It aims to inform, educate and enlighten readers about Africa through twenty-six African related characters. The book is essentially an A-Z resource book on Africa.

The books listed above are available on Amazon in both paperback and ebook formats.

THE REAL ABOLITIONISTS

Resistance and Rebellion in the Face of Slavery

Respect Due Vol. 1

MICHAEL NATHAN-PEPPLE

Copyright © 2025 Michael Nathan-Pepple
Published by Michael Nathan-Pepple
For enquiries email: mnathanpepple@gmail.com

The right of the author to be identified as the Author
of this Work have been asserted in accordance with
the Copyright, Designs and Patents Act 1988.

All rights reserved. No part of this publication may be
reproduced, stored in a retrieval system or transmitted, in any
forms or by any means, electronic, mechanical, photocopying
or otherwise, without the prior permission of the publisher.

ISBN: 978-1-9162807-3-1

DEDICATION

The book is dedicated to the millions of enslaved Africans (men, women and children) who survived the horrendous Middle Passage and endured the savagery and trauma of racialised chattel slavery in the hands of white Europeans. Many of these lives will never be known, but this book celebrates their existence. May their souls continue to rest in peace and power!

CONTENTS

Dedication	5
List Of Illustrations	9
Preface	13
Horrors of Slavery and Reparations	15
Introduction	22

CHAPTER ONE

African Resistance to Slavery	26
Slave ship revolts	29
Resistance and Rebellion in the Americas	32

CHAPTER TWO

Enslaved Narrators	40
Ignatius Sancho (1729-1780)	40
Ottobah Cugoano (c.1757-after 1791)	42
Olaudah Equiano (c.1745-1797)	45
Mary Prince (c.1788-after 1833)	48
Sojourner Truth (1797-1883)	51
Frederick Douglass (1818-1895)	53
Harriet Tubman (1822-1913)	57

CHAPTER THREE

Rebel Leaders   64

Gaspar Yanga (1545-after 1618)   64

Benkos Biohó (late 1500s-1621)   66

King Cuffy [Cuffee or Kofi] of Barbados (Unknown-Unknown)   70

Ganga Zumbi (1655-1694)   72

Prince Klaas [Kwaku Takyi] aka King Court (c.1690-1736)   76

Francois Mackandal (unknown-1758)   79

Nanny of the Maroons (c.1686-c.1760)   81

Bokilifu Boni (1730-1793)   84

Gabriel Prosser (1776-1800)   87

Toussaint L'Ouverture (1743-1803)   90

Jean-Jacques Dessalines (1758-1806)   93

Marcos Xiorro (unknown-unknown)   97

Nat Turner (1800-1831)   100

Samuel Sharpe (c.1801-1832)   102

Carlota Lukumi (unknown-1843)   105

CHAPTER FOUR

Conclusion   112

Records of Some Slave Revolts in the Americas   117

Bibliography   121

LIST OF ILLUSTRATIONS

Atrocities of Slavery	21
The Gate [Door] of No Return	24
Treaty of Tordesillas	28
The Triangular Trade	28
From Capture to Slave Ship Revolt	31
Images of Slave Rebellions	36
Portraits of Enslaved Narrators	61
Statues of Rebel Leaders	109
Statute of Bussa of Barbados	116

A statement by the Ndyuka-Maroon paramount leader, Granman Gazon Matodja, [Suriname]

NOVEMBER 5, 1998.

We, the Ndyuka people, have been living in the interior of Suriname for centuries. From the very first moments of our arrival in what is now called Suriname, we fought against the whites and freed ourselves from the inhumane system of slavery. Slavery was a degradation of human life and human values. Human beings were turned into working machines. The only way people could free themselves from that system was to be courageous and not to be afraid to sacrifice their lives. Even mothers and children had to sacrifice their lives. Indeed, it is true that we paid a high price for our freedom. At no price are we going to let the government take it away today. This freedom is enshrined in the treaty with the whites.

Everyone who denies the value of the treaty denies the slavery that was imposed on the children of Africa, denies the hardships that we endured during slavery, denies our freedom and our existence as human beings. In my understanding this treaty is still valid even though there is no slavery anymore. How could one deny this treaty, which we shed so much blood for? How could I deny my history? How could I throw away the bonds between the present and the past, between past generations and those of the present?

During slavery the whites had their laws, but we had our own laws too. The laws of the whites were made to oppress us, to justify and even promote slavery (evil). We had and still have laws to govern ourselves. Our laws allow us to live in peace and harmony.

We did not gain our freedom by the laws of the whites, as did most of the other peoples in Suriname. Today [the government of Suriname imposes] rules on us, and expect us to respect and abide by them. They deny everything we achieved in the past, but they need to understand that the treaty existed a long time before the laws we have now. We are not going to give up what we achieved in the past at any price.

PREFACE

This book was written to bridge several historical gaps, particularly those related to slavery in the Americas and the roles played by some notable abolitionists, who were first and foremost, enslaved Africans. While European writers throughout history have conveyed the idea that a number of prominent white people were the only abolitionists, it is important to emphasise that they joined the struggle long after black people had begun to fight for their liberation.

The Real Abolitionists focuses on recognising, after much research, some of the enslaved Africans and their descendants, who fought tirelessly and bravely in an attempt to liberate themselves and millions of others from the brutality of chattel slavery. Although it was not a structured or coordinated movement with all the trappings of wealth and influence, as was the case when Europeans began campaigning to end the slave trade in the late 1700s (final decades of the 18th century), it was made up of ordinary men and women who desired freedom and were willing to die for it.

Given that this type of history is poorly documented in colonial documents and has never been fully taught in educational institutions both past and present, it is not surprising that many people are unaware of what happened during the dark days of the trans-Atlantic slave trade and the subsequent chattel slavery system. The article *Horrors of Slavery and Reparations* was included in the book to shed light on the abuse of millions of enslaved Africans who are no longer alive to tell their own horror stories, and why reparations are necessary.

In essence, the book illustrates the struggle for liberation by enslaved Africans and their descendants, as well as the triumph of the human spirit over adversity. This is also an opportunity to thank everyone who has contributed or written on this subject. We must continue to seek the truth, since the truth is what will set us all free. Additionally, I want to thank my wife, Sheralyn Nathan-Pepple, for her support and for taking on the role as the main proof reader.

Michael Nathan-Pepple

HORRORS OF SLAVERY AND REPARATIONS

Oh the horrors of slavery! - How the thought of it pains my heart! But the truth ought to be told of it; and what my eyes have seen I think it is my duty to relate; for few people in England [World] know what slavery is. I have been a slave - I have felt what a slave feels, and I know what a slave knows; and I would have all the good people in England [World] to know it too, that they may break our chains, and set us free.

— MARY PRINCE

Many of the *Slave narratives* discussed in this book tell the stories of enslaved Africans and their descendants. They are inspirational, historically significant and effective in the fight against slavery. The authors of these fascinating stories, all of whom were once enslaved, such as Frederick Douglass, Sojourner Truth, Olaudah Equiano, Ottobah Cugoano, Mary Prince and many others, shared their personal accounts of the horrors and savage acts inflicted on them and millions of others who did nothing wrong except be from Africa or descended from it and have black or brown skin. These narratives gave enslaved people a sense of humanity and self-worth while also documenting their oral expressions of suffering. Many of the events expressed in these narratives are too graphic and distressing to be included in this book. Therefore, I strongly advise readers to conduct additional research to get a true and complete picture of what transpired during the trans-Atlantic slave trade and the evil period of chattel slavery that followed in the *New World* (aka the Americas, which includes North, Central and South America, and the islands of the Caribbean, aka West Indies).

In recent years, descendants of enslaved Africans have stepped up their demands for reparations. However, some people, both whites and, regrettably, blacks, have refused to support this action, citing reasons why they should not be paid. These deniers of an experience that decimated enslaved people's cultures, languages, history and way of life must examine their conscience. The truth is that Africans were kidnapped from their homes, forcibly shipped to the Americas, sold as commodities to provide free labour to European plantation owners and subjected to the most heinous violence, discrimination and racism imaginable. Furthermore, the plantation owner (aka enslaver) had complete control over the enslaved people's physical, mental and cultural well-being. Several historical records clearly show that enslaved Africans were brutally treated, reduced to the status of two-legged animals, branded like cattle with the enslaver's initials on their arms, chest, forehead or back, and denied all rights to their humanity, heritage, beliefs and values, or family connections. It is not an exaggeration to state that enslaved Africans were treated worse than animals across the Americas. Ironically, it seemed absurd that people who committed such atrocious crimes against millions of enslaved Africans went unpunished. It is both frightening and sad that the psychopathic slave/plantation owners, as well as the slave-trading nations that supported them, were motivated solely by power, control, sugar addiction, profit and greed. In doing so, they established an industrialised global capitalist system that allowed them to amass enormous wealth. Astonishingly, enslaved Africans who escaped or attempted to escape slavery were considered as having a mental illness called *Drapetomania*. The term was described as a *psychological disorder* and invented by Samuel Adolphus Cartwright, an American physician in 1851. It makes one wonder who genuinely had the mental disorder.

In reality, many European settlers in the Americas were unwilling or lazy to work and believed that exploiting African slave labour would significantly increase their personal wealth. For example, after being advised to abandon the concept of slavery, early settlers in the colony of Georgia in the United States of America (USA), aka the United States (US), "began to grumble that they would never make money unless they were allowed to employ enslaved Africans" (Wood, 2002). Under chattel slavery, enslaved Africans were not legally recognised as human beings and were treated cruelly. The intention of this slavery system was to render them all faceless, voiceless and cultureless. In terms of sustainability, they were only fed non-nutritional foods in order to keep them alive. After slavery was abolished in the various jurisdictions, slave-trading nations, such as Britain (1834 and 1838), France (1848) and the United States (1865), compensated slave owners, while the victims of their dreadful crimes, whose free labour contributed significantly to their prosperity, received nothing, not even assistance during the transition to freedom. How can this be fair? Furthermore, enslaved people in Spanish-controlled territories in the Americas were expected to pay for their freedom through a self-purchase by instalment system known as *coartación*, despite the fact that they should have been the ones compensated. In addition, following the success of the Haitian revolution in 1804, the French government demanded payment from the newly liberated Haitians in exchange for their freedom or recognition of independence.

From 1835 to 1843, the British government paid a staggering £20 million (£17 billion today) in compensation to slave owners for the loss of *property*. Yes, people of African descent (or Black people) were treated as property. The vast majority of this money was returned to their ancestral family homes in Europe and used to fund businesses and projects, as well as to better their own and their descendants' lives. Those who say that slavery is a thing of the past and that reparations are unnecessary should remember that the money paid to British slave owners was a loan from investors, which was managed by the Bank of England on behalf of the government. This money was only repaid in

2015, after years of taxing the British public, including descendants of enslaved people. To be honest, the demand for reparations by the descendants of enslaved Africans is very minimal, given what their ancestors went through for over four centuries, and the impact is still felt today. Some may ask who should be held responsible for reparations. In truth, that is not a mystery because information on British recipients of slave compensation was published in the 1837-8 Parliamentary Papers, which included Members of British Parliament, Bank of England directors, and peers and barons from British elite families. To answer the question and according to international law, it is the state, individuals, institutions and corporations that owned, caused suffering and profited from the enslavement and labour of Africans.

So, for a slave-trading nation like Britain to portray itself as benevolent liberators of Africans while ignoring its role as the world's leading slave-trading nation can only be interpreted as an attempt to distance itself from the trans-Atlantic slave trade, which brutalised, exploited and dehumanised Black people. According to David and Richardson (2010) as cited in Equal Justice Initiative (2023), "ships originating in Great Britain were responsible for trafficking more than a quarter of all people taken from Africa from 1501 to 1867." Moreover, by the end of the 18th century, Britain had taken on a dominant role, controlling almost 40% of European slave trading on the African coast. The Netherlands (aka Holland), did not miss out on compensating slave owners. After slavery was abolished in 1863, the Dutch government compensated owners with 300 guilders per slave. In the United States, three months before the Civil War ended in April 1865, an attempt was made to make some form of reparations to newly freed enslaved people. This involved the issuance of an order granting them 400,000 acres of coastal land from Charleston, South Carolina to the St. John's River in Florida. These were to be divided into 40-acre plots for their sole and exclusive use. The army was later directed to lend mules to the freedmen, hence the phrase *40 acres and a mule*. Following Abraham Lincoln's assassination on April 14, 1865, Vice

President Andrew Johnson revoked the order upon becoming President, and all future requests for reparations were never considered.

More recently, the Portuguese, the first European nation to begin enslaving Africans, publicly stated that "it has no plans to pay reparations for the country's role in transatlantic slavery and colonialism" (Roberts, 2024). This statement was made after Portugal's debate over colonial and slavery reparations resurfaced in 2024. Every African descendant or black person should be concerned about the trend and outright refusal of former slave-trading European nations (including the USA) and institutions to formally apologise, let alone pay reparations. It sends the wrong message to potential abusers and exploiters, implying that they can commit such atrocious crimes against fellow humans and get away with it. Consequently, reparation or reparatory justice is an absolute requirement that must be met in order to prevent chattel slavery and all other forms of slavery from ever happening again. As the late Dr. Martin Luther King Jr. famously said, *Injustice anywhere is a threat to justice everywhere.*

Reparations are more than just about money, as many people believe; it begins with telling the truth, admitting historical wrongs and making genuine amends. This will result in justice that honours the memory of the dead and empowers the living, while also opening the door to reconciliation and healing. Hilary Beckles, head of the Caribbean Community political and economic union (CARICOM) reparations commission, stated at a news conference following a joint meeting with the African Union calling for reparations for slavery that "humanity cannot go forward with all the toxic interferences of colonization...we have to clean up this mess to allow humanity to function." (Demony, 2023). Moreover, the concept of reparation is not new to humanity, and there is documented evidence that many countries have paid reparations for atrocities far less severe [but still significant] than those committed against enslaved Africans and their descendants. According to a 2014 article, the U.S. government paid reparations to Japanese Americans under the Japanese-American

Claims Act of 1948 ($38 million between 1948 and 1965) and the Civil Liberties Act of 1988 ($20,000 cash payment to each survivor) for wrongfully keeping 120,000 people in internment camps during World War II. The article also stated that during the same war, "Germany paid reparations to Holocaust victims, and gave Israel $7 billion as the nation was forming. By 2012, the German government had paid $89 billion in reparations to individual survivors as well" (Matthews, 2014). Therefore, there is precedent in giving reparations to victims of crime, abuse and exploitation.

> *"We [the descendants of enslaved Africans] owe it to ourselves and future generations of humanity to ensure that the trans-Atlantic slave trade and the enslavement of Africans in the Caribbean, Latin, central, south and north America is accepted as a crime against humanity, and that the appropriate apology and compensation is paid, and that the international community accepts that this should never happen again."*
> —PRIME MINISTER DICKON MITCHELL OF GRENADA (20 FEBRUARY, 2025)

ATROCITIES OF SLAVERY

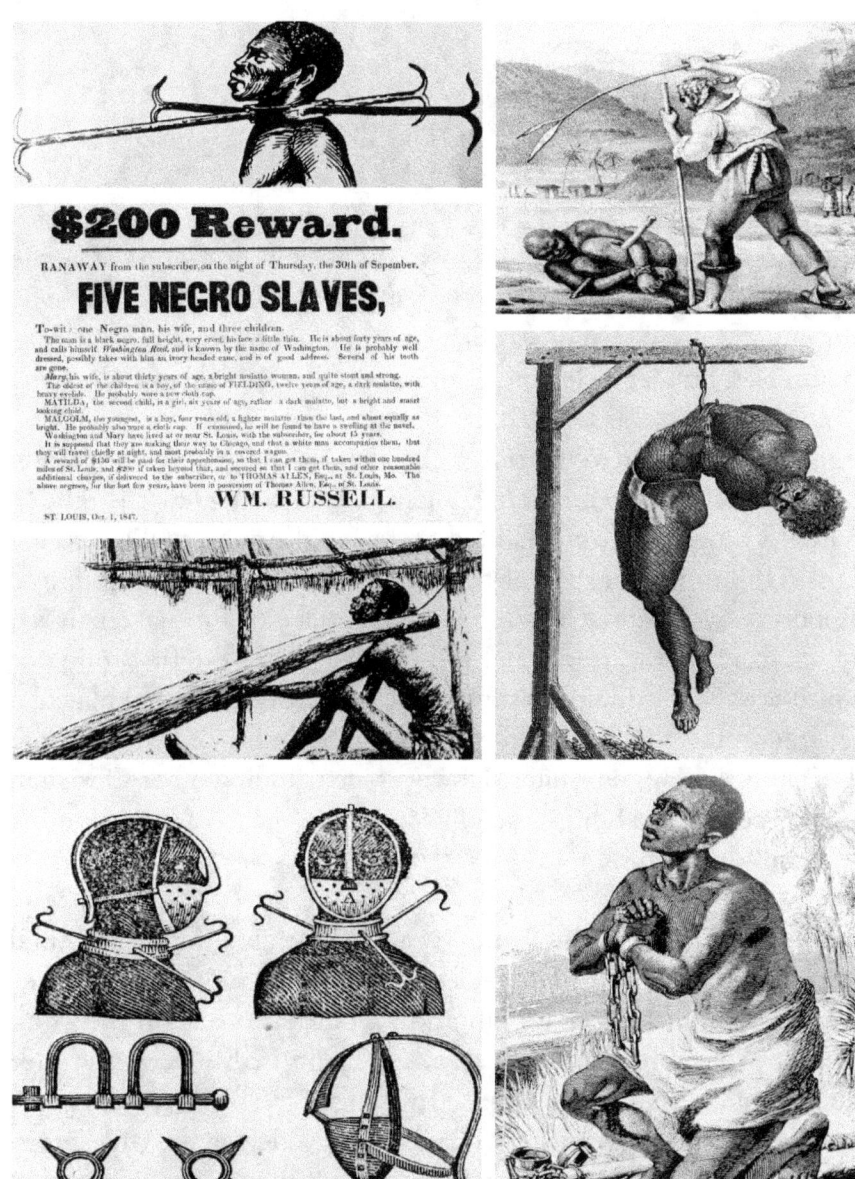

*Despite the cruel treatment of enslaved Africans,
their spirits remained unbroken*

INTRODUCTION

Many people define an abolitionist as a person or group of people who wanted to end the enslavement of Africans in the Americas. The movement to end slavery was first championed by enslaved Africans themselves, but centuries later (around the 1780s and beyond), some prominent Europeans joined the fight, including Thomas Clarkson (England), William Wilberforce (England), Granville Sharp (England), Jacques Pierre Brissot (France), Victor Schoelcher (France), William Lloyd Garrison (United States) and Anna Amalia Bergendahl (Holland). Because of their white skin, social standing and support networks, they became the public face of anti-slavery movements. It is worth noting that the Quakers were the first religious group to take a principled stand against slavery, and they played a key role in the abolitionist movements in both the United Kingdom (UK) and the United States. However, as with any other Christian religious denomination, some of its members owned a large number of enslaved Africans.

While not all sympathetic Europeans or white abolitionists favoured complete liberation for enslaved Africans, some preferred that they stay on plantations as paid labourers in order to sustain the enormously profitable sugar industry. Others argued that, while slave labour would eventually disappear, rushing to freedom would deprive slave owners of their *property*. However, considering the widespread prejudice displayed by most whites at the time, it is reasonable to assume that those who advocated for enslaved people's emancipation were less likely to treat them as equals. Moreover, many white abolitionists criticised and lamented over the frequency of slave revolts (aka rebellions, uprisings, mutinies and insurrections), but they were unable to distant themselves from the rebels because they were fighting for the same cause. Even though some white people saw the evils of slavery, the struggle was much more personal for black abolitionists, who were more concerned with action than rhetoric in the fight for freedom.

This is the first book in a two-part series called *Respect Due*. It seeks to correct historical misinformation. The book *The Real Abolitionists* will show how enslaved Africans in the Americas fought relentlessly for their freedom. Unfortunately, their struggles to free themselves from bondage have received not much attention. Though many lives were lost, these freedom fighters were the first to dispel the myths that Africans just accepted the servitude nature of slavery and would forever be the beasts of burden for Caucasians (white people). In fact, slave resistance occurred wherever slavery existed. Enslaved Africans and their descendants used their strategic skills to fight the slave system, as well as their intelligence to effectively argue for the abolition of slavery. These efforts had a considerable impact on pressuring European slave owners and their supporting governments that slavery was becoming unsustainable. Even after slavery was eventually abolished across the Americas, African descendants and black people in general have continue to live with many of the racist myths that were used to justify the trans-Atlantic slave trade and subsequent chattel slavery system. Finally, the book serves as a starting point for further research for anyone interested in learning about and understanding the origins of many of the challenges facing people of African descent today.

The Gate [Door] of No Return, Cape Coast Castle, Ghana

CHAPTER ONE

AFRICAN RESISTANCE TO SLAVERY

African resistance to the infamous trans-Atlantic slave trade began almost immediately after its inception in the early 1500s. However, the European slave trade in Africa, which later evolved into the trans-Atlantic slave trade (aka Triangle trade), started in 1441, when 12 Africans from present-day Mauritania were kidnapped, taken to Portugal and sold as slaves. Three years later (1444), another 235 kidnapped Africans arrived in the southern Portuguese town of Lagos. During the early days of slavery, the Portuguese raided coastal towns and villages with the help of seamen from the Republic of Genoa (now part of present-day Italy) to capture these Africans. However, European merchants changed tactics and persuaded African kings and chiefs to sell them their prisoners of war (mainly from rival ethnic groups) or those being held as punishment for certain crimes, along with agricultural produce, ivory and gold. Subsequently, Lisbon, the capital of Portugal, became Europe's main trading centre for enslaved Africans. This resulted in the forcible transportation of thousands of African captives to the Iberian Peninsula (present-day Spain and Portugal). In the early 16th century, 10% of Lisbon's population was of African descent, and by the mid-16th century, 20% of births in Palos de la Frontera, Spain, were black (Sherwood, 1992).

Prior to the arrival of Africans in the Americas, and after Pope Alexander VI had divided the world outside of Europe into two (under the Papal bull, *Inter Caetera* in 1493 and the signing of the *Treaty of Tordesillas* by Portugal and Spain in 1494), giving the eastern part to Portugal and the western part to Spain, Europeans went on a rampage and massacred the vast majority of the indigenous population in the Americas. They violently colonised territories (amounting to 42.55 million square kilometres or 16,428,000 square miles) owned and occupied by various groups, such as the Inuit (usually called *Eskimos* by Europeans), Iroquois, Apache, Cherokee, Seminole, Miskito, Arawak, Taino, Maya, Inca and Aztec. According to Everett (1978), a judge wrote in 1518, "When Hispaniola was discovered, it contained 1.3 million Indians; today their number does not exceed 11, 000." Furthermore, a 2019 University of London (UK) study found that over 100 years (1492-1600) after European arrival, about 56 million people out of a population of 60 million were ruthlessly killed as a result of warfare and slavery, or died from European diseases, such as smallpox, measles, influenza and cholera. This represents 90% of the population and is referred to in the study as the *Great Dying*. In addition, all of the major empires and civilisations established by indigenous peoples of the Americas hundreds of years before European colonists arrived were completely destroyed. The genocide of the indigenous population, resulted in the arrival of millions of African captives who had been trafficked from their homes across Africa, from the West coast to the East coast, including Congo and Angola in Central Africa and the West-Central Coast of Southern Africa. In order to maintain their dignity and humanity, these African captives resisted on slave ships, sought various escape routes once in the Americas and organised numerous forms of resistance that terrified enslavers and kept them awake at night.

Several accounts of these early outbreaks revealed that during more than 400 years of European incursion on the African coast, Africans used their fighting spirit and stamina to attack, resist and disrupt this inhumane trade. These ideals were reaffirmed in a speech by Dr Keith Rowley, former Prime Minister of Trinidad and Tobago (T&T's) during the opening of the Emancipation Day procession on August 1, 2023, when he quoted CLR James, one of T&T's notable literary figures, as saying, "African slaves fought back, powerfully, with the contents of their minds - the memories, logic, and resilience of their people." (Polo, 2023). In the same speech, Rowley referred to

Treaty of Tordesillas: *An agreement that endorsed the Pope dividing the world into two parts*

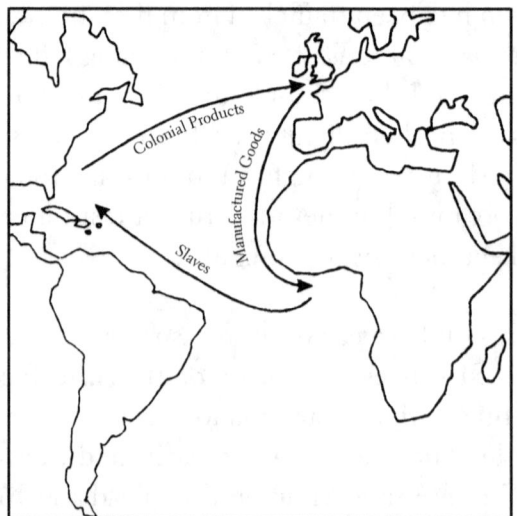

The Triangular Trade: *Ships would leave Europe with textiles, manufactured goods, including weapons and alcohol, which they would sell in Africa before travelling to the New World with a cargo of enslaved people to be exchanged for colonial produce (sugar, coffee, tobacco, etc).*

enslaved descendants as victims of the African *cultural holocaust* and criticised those who have spoken out against paying reparations to descendants of African slaves. For those unfamiliar with this part of African slavery history, the fight against slavery began in the interior of Africa, which was the initial point of capture for many captives. It then moved to the coast and eventually reached places off the coast of Africa, such as the islands of Madeira, Canary Islands, Cape Verde, Fernando Po (now Bioko) and São Tomé and Príncipe. For instance, Cape Verde, mainly the islands of Santiago and Fogo, served as a major hub for slave traffickers who transported enslaved Africans to Europe, other Atlantic islands and the Americas.

Slave ship revolts

The bloody revolts or mutinies on slave ships were among the first attempts taken by Africans to resist being sent to a horrible fate across the Atlantic. Such resistance ranged from a single act of defiance, an isolated act of violence, or a deadly attempt to jump overboard to massive revolts that erupted into a life-or-death confrontation between African captives and European sailors. The Africans defended themselves against excessive abuse despite being crammed and chained together, with each person occupying a space no larger than a coffin. The struggle for freedom continued unabatedly, and those who rebelled were savagely punished, with ringleaders murdered in front of other captives. The first recorded slave ship revolt happened in 1532, when 109 enslaved Africans on a Portuguese ship rose up and killed the whole crew, with the exception of the pilot and two seamen. A similar incident took place off the coast of Ecuador in 1650, when a slave ship sank. The captives wasted no time in eliminating the remaining Spanish crew. In June 1730, after days of sailing from the coast of Guinea, a group of African captives aboard an Atlantic slave ship *Little George* escaped, seized weapons and killed several crew members, while the captain and the rest of the crew surrendered. Despite their lack of sailing skills, the captured Africans successfully turned the ship around and returned to the shores of Sierra Leone. The captain of the ship, George Scott, later described the revolt in great detail. Another example of a slave ship insurrection occurred in 1742, when locals forced the *Galley Mary* (a ship propelled mostly by oars) ashore on the Gambian river. The captives on board murdered the majority of the crew and held the captain for 27 days. In 1752, African captives on the *Marlborough* also freed themselves while at sea. After killing the majority of the crew, they forced those remaining to ship them back to Africa.

The fight for freedom by Africans was continuous, as was evidenced by a remarkable event in 1803, when a group of Igbo [also spelt Ebo or Ibo] (West African tribe) captives gained control of the vessel and drowned their captors. After the landing, they walked off the ship and committed mass suicide in the marshy waters of Dunbar Creek on St. Simons Island, Georgia (USA). This incident revealed that Africans would rather die and have their souls return to their ancestral land in Africa than suffer the misery of slavery. The *Amistad* Mutiny, which occurred on July 1, 1839, is one of the most famous slave rebellions onboard a slave ship. It involved 53 African captives kidnapped in Sierra Leone and taken to Havana, Cuba, a slave trade centre. On their journey to the designated plantation, they seized the ship, killed the captain and cook, and demanded that the remaining crew members return them to Africa. Despite being deceived and carried to Long Island, New York, they were arrested by the US Navy, tried, won their case, and returned to Africa. The film Amistad, which premiered in 1997, tells the true story. The events surrounding the Amistad story received little attention at the time, which clearly demonstrated that Africans would not allow oppressors to devalue their customs and culture, but would instead resist and fight back.

The voyages from Africa to the Americas (aka the Middle Passage) took between six and twelve weeks, depending on weather condition and distance to cover. Approximately 20% or one-fifth of the 12 to 20 million African captives who were transported as *human cargo*

FROM CAPTURE TO SLAVE SHIP REVOLT

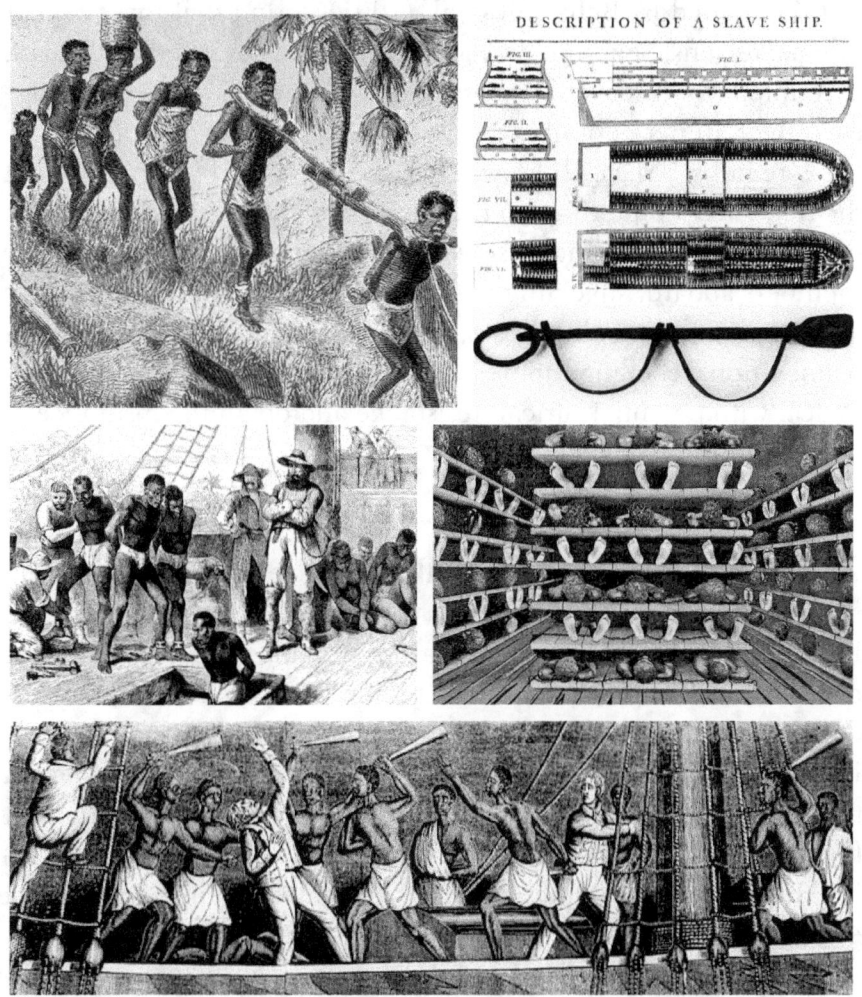

"If you enslave a proud nation, rebellion becomes their right"

died during the treacherous journey (Sherman-Peter, 2022). Experts studying historical data calculated that there were almost 500 documented acts of revolts on slave ship between 1650 and 1860, with majority taking place at sea, just off the West coast of Africa. However, it is estimated that as many as one in ten slave ships experienced a revolt, [over the entire history of the trans-Atlantic slave trade], with many of these incidents going unreported. Marcum and Skarbek (2014) as cited by Behrendt et al. (2001), found that three Upper Guinea regions, Senegambia, Sierra Leone and the Windward Coast, accounted "for just over 10 per cent of the slaves leaving Africa; however, over 40 per cent of the voyages with slave revolts came from these regions." Slave ship owners were also clearly worried about the frequency of mutinies on their ships and, as a result, took drastic measures to prevent them, such as increasing the number of crew members aboard, shackling adult males with chains and padlocks and keeping them below decks, erecting wooden barriers to protect seamen from rebelling captives, redesigning and organising the ships to deal with potential African resistance and obtaining insurance to cover mutiny losses.

Resistance and Rebellion in the Americas

Resistance and Rebellion by enslaved Africans was a key feature of chattel slavery in the Americas. Based on historical records, the first documented large scale rebellion of enslaved Africans took place in December 1521 on the Spanish colony of Santo Domingo, located on the Island of La Espanola (later called Hispaniola). Despite the fact that marronage (the act of escaping slavery) first appeared in Spanish Hispaniola in 1503, the governor "was already complaining that escaped slaves could not be retrieved and were teaching the Taino Indians bad customs" (Landers, no date). To show the gravity of marronage, which Thompson (2006) describes as "an extreme form of resistance," the Spanish authorities issued decrees against rebellious slaves as early as 1525.

Although not all of the rebellions where successful, several are worth highlighting based on where or when they occurred and their significance at the time, such as the 1526 San Miguel de Gualdape Rebellion (near present day Sapelo Island, Georgia, USA); the 1570

AFRICAN RESISTANCE TO SLAVERY

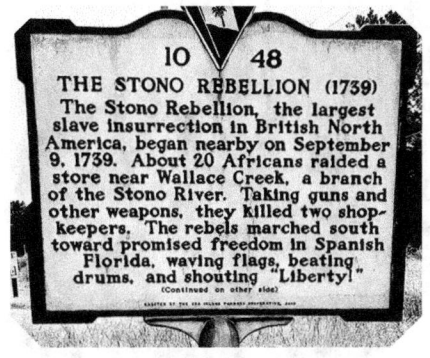

Historical Highway Marker Listing of The Stone Rebellion

Gaspar Yanga's Revolt (Mexico); the 1656 Slave Revolt (Guadeloupe); the 1675 Barbados Slave Rebellion; the 1712 New York City Slave Revolt (USA); the 1728-1739 Maroon Wars (Jamaica); the 1733-1734 St. John Revolt (US Virgin Island); the 1739 Stono Rebellion, South Carolina (USA); the 1760-1761 Tacky Rebellion (Jamaica); the 1763 Berbice Revolt (Guyana); the 1765-1793 Boni Maroon Wars (Suriname); the 1770 Sandy's Rebellion (Tobago); and the 1791-1804 Saint-Domingue aka Haitian Revolution (Haiti). The latter resulted in the establishment of an independent black state, inspired revolts throughout the Caribbean and Americas, and was the most successful slave rebellion in history.

Between the 16th and 18th centuries, enslaved Africans and their descendants established numerous independent Maroon (derived from the Spanish word *cimarrón* [*wild* or *untamed*] and used to describe Africans who had escaped slavery) communities in several countries, including Jamaica, Haiti, Cuba, St. Vincent, Peru, Dominica, Guyana, Mexico, Brazil, Colombia, Ecuador, Suriname, French Guiana (aka Guyane), Guadeloupe, Venezuela, Honduras, Puerto Rico, Barbados, Panama, US Virgin Islands (St. John and St. Thomas), Canada (Halifax and Nova Scotia), and parts of the United States, such as Texas and Florida, and the Great Dismal Swamp, on the Virginia and North Carolina border. In British North America and the USA alone, "over 50 Maroon settlements [were] established between 1672 and 1864" (Connell, 2017).

During the era of slavery in the Americas, Maroon groups ranging in size from small bands to powerful states sent revolutionary shockwaves throughout the plantocracy system, exposing the lie of

European racial superiority. Many of these groups intermarried with indigenous Amerindian tribes, forming alliances to defend themselves against militia and troops sent by European colonisers and invaders. However, there were numerous cases in which Amerindians collaborated with Europeans to apprehend runaway Africans. Additionally, the role of enslaved African women in marronage, as well as their success in sustaining Maroon communities, is often overlooked. Despite the historical dominance of men in Maroon leadership, certain women have been recognised as heroines, such as Jamaica's legendary Queen Nanny, Guadeloupe's Solitude, St. Lucia's Flore Bois Gaillard, St. John's [Danish: St. Jan] (US Virgin Island) Breffu and Haiti's Marie-Jeanne Lamartiniére. These remarkable women escaped slavery, rose to the ranks of military leadership and fought for their own and their people's freedom.

Statue of Solitude of Guadeloupe - In 1802, She Helped Lead A Slave Revolt While 8 Months Pregnant

The majority of maroon women engaged in a range of community-building duties, including growing food crops, feeding the community, reproducing the maroon population, reviving African cultural and religious practices as teachers and priestesses, and fighting alongside their men. In essence, without women's contributions, many Maroon societies would not have survived. According to Thompson (2006), "Maroon children stood a better chance than other Black children of being brought up in a wholesome environment and being cared for directly by their parents." Even though people in maroon communities spoke different African languages and came from diverse ethnicities and backgrounds, they were able to coexist and overcome enormous challenges. This was because they viewed their inter-ethnic alliances as sources of strength, not weakness. Their continuous existence as distinct ethnic and cultural communities shows the courage, determination and commitment that have sustained them for centuries while keeping the African spirit and influence.

In the period aptly described as the Age of Revolution (late 18th to mid-19th century), enslaved Africans and their descendants recorded the most frequent, best known and largest slave revolts and conspiracies in the Americas. Ironically, these waves of revolutionary actions happened at the same time as events in Europe and among whites in the USA. Two of the most significant of these conflicts were the American Revolution (1765-1783) and the French Revolution (1789-1799). It is assumed that the outbreak of these events served as inspiration for some of the intense revolutionary activities that emerged from enslaved African communities. Furthermore, historians of enslavement in the Western Hemisphere have discovered a strong link between the mass arrivals of African captives and the emergence of insurgencies and revolts in the Americas. For example, in 1790, "African-born slaves made up about 60% of Saint-Domingue's population" (Girard, 2012). This demonstrates that the closer enslaved people of African descent were to their own cultures and customs, the greater their desire and motivation to fight for their freedom. The most widespread and long-lasting of these conflicts occurred when emancipated slaves refused to be re-enslaved, as in St. Lucia (1795-97), Saint-Domingue/Haiti (after 1793) and Guadeloupe (1802). Essentially, the Age of Revolution was a time when the abolitionist movement's voice, both white and black, grew louder, drowning out that of plantation owners and supporters.

Enslaved Africans fought for their freedom in a variety of ways other than violence (physical rebellions). In the late 18th century, a number of Africans and African descendants authored or dictated their powerful stories to educate the public by highlighting and promoting the message of abolition. For example, Olaudah Equiano (aka

IMAGES OF SLAVE REBELLIONS

*Freedom is never voluntarily given by the oppressor;
it must be demanded by the oppressed."*
—MARTIN LUTHER KING JR.

Gustavus Vassa) wrote his autobiography, *The Interesting Narrative of the Life of Olaudah Equiano*, which was published in London in 1789. Other former enslaved people who used their stories or narratives to convey the evil nature of slavery and thus justify, promote and support the abolitionist movement included Harriet Jacobs, Ottobah Cugoano, Mary Prince, Frederick Douglass, Moses Roper, Josiah Henson, William Wells Brown and Solomon Northup, whose autobiography *Twelve Years a Slave*, published in 1858, was adapted into an Oscar-winning film in 2013. The experiences they revealed provided a tangible tool for the abolition movement while also dispelling certain misunderstandings about the slave trade and slavery.

The most common form of resistance to slavery was the day-to-day resistance, which included deliberate slow working, faking illness, sabotage of machinery or tools, and running away for short periods of time in response to the enslavers' abuse. The vast majority of enslaved people committed these acts as isolated incidents intended to disrupt the plantation's daily routine in any way possible. Some observers may have perceived these types of offenses as destabilising or a way to relieve stress, but the consequences for an enslaved person were typically horrific and cruel. For example, they were castrated, violently flogged, locked up for days without water in an oven-like hothouse, shackled or forced to wear a ball and chain for weeks, had limbs amputated (particularly the foot), placed on stakes and slowly burned alive, hanged, shot, and even sold. However, some choose to defy enslavement by suicide and self-mutilation. Before slavery was abolished in the United States, there were over 250 documented slave revolts or attempted revolts involving ten or more enslaved people. These incidents were particularly common in the Caribbean and South America, where the resistance sought to destroy or reduce the efficiency of the slavery system.

"History, despite its wrenching pain, cannot be unlived,
but if faced with courage, need not be lived again."
—MAYA ANGELOU

"Better to die fighting for freedom than be
a prisoner all the days of your life."
—BOB MARLEY

CHAPTER TWO

ENSLAVED NARRATORS

Ignatius Sancho (1729-1780)

Ignatius Sancho was a multi-talented person who worked as a playwright, composer, theatre critic, shopkeeper, and an activists against racism and slavery. Throughout his lifetime, he was referred to as *the extraordinary Negro*, representing African humanity to those opposed to the slave trade. Sancho was born on a ship in the Middle Passage in 1729. The ship was transporting African captives from West Africa to the Spanish colony of New Granada (present-day Colombia, Panama, Ecuador and Venezuela). His enslaved parents died when he was a baby, leaving him an orphan. In order to avoid the atrocities of slavery, his father committed suicide, and his mother passed away from an illness. Sancho's owner brought him to Greenwich, England, when he was two years old, and he was given as a gift to three unmarried sisters as their *slave*. The sisters gave him the surname Sancho because he resembled a servant of someone they knew. While growing up in the sisters' household, the 2nd Duke of Montagu, a neighbour, noticed Sancho's intelligence. The Duke encouraged him to read, write and possibly play a musical instrument. Interestingly, the three sisters opposed Sancho's education, claiming that ignorance was the best and only guarantee of obedience.

When Sancho turned 20, after the Duke's death, he approached his widow for a job and was employed as a butler. He worked for the Duchess until her death in 1751, when he was granted his freedom and went to work for the 1st Duke of Montagu. Sancho married Anne Osborne, a *West Indian* woman of African descent, in 1758, and they had seven children. While serving as a valet (a gentleman's male servant) for the Duke, Sancho got the opportunity to have his portrait painted by Thomas Gainsborough, one of Britain's most famous portrait and landscape painters of the 18th century. In addition, he began to participate in the city's artistic and cultural scene, and became known for writing letters to record his thoughts on issues concerning the late 18th-century Britain and its empire. By 1773, Sancho was unable to meet the demands of his job, so he left the Montagus household to open a grocery store in Westminster with his wife. The store was funded through his personal savings and some financial assistance from the Montagu family.

Sancho's store sold a variety of necessities, such as sugar, tea and tobacco. In addition to buying essentials, many of his customers sought advice and companionship. Aside from running his store, he was politically active, composed and published his own music, wrote numerous letters to correspondents and newspapers, and maintained contact with friends and associates. The majority of his letters were written during the last five years of his life (1775-1780), and the topics ranged from the realities of family life to the plight of enslaved Black people around the world, and, most importantly, the abolition of slavery. Sancho also wrote about the horrors of slavery and racism in Britain during the mid-to-late1700s slavery debates, when the country had become the world's leading slave-trading nation. In a protest letter to the renowned white novelist and clergyman Laurence Sterne in 1766, Sancho urged him to devote time to writing about the abolition of slavery. His only published work during his lifetime were five volumes of his original musical compositions, which appeared between 1767 and 1779. Furthermore, despite the fact that only 3% of the population was eligible to vote, Sancho used his property ownership rights by voting in the general elections of 1774 and 1780. This made him the first person of African descent to vote in Britain. Other firsts associated with Sancho included the first black British composer, the first African prose writer published in England and the first black man whose obituary was published in British newspapers.

The majority of information about Sancho's life comes from Joseph Jekyll's 1782 biography and, to a lesser extent, a collection of his letters published in 1782 in the volume *Letters of the late Ignatius Sancho, an African* (henceforth *Letters*) by Francis Crewe, Sancho's friend. Some have questioned Jekyll's biography of Sancho, citing inconsistencies with the events described in *Letters*. Many have questioned his sources. Critics of *Letters* argue that "Crewe's 127-word preface does not provide Sancho's purpose and does not invite readers to engage directly with his voice in Letters." (Tita, 2023). Both publications were seen as undermining the accurate representation of Sancho's letters, distorting his true vision and artistic brilliance. Nonetheless, Ignatius Sancho's letters are regarded as an excellent example of African literature. Sancho was a proud African writer, recognised as a *man of letters*, who used his wits, intelligence and extensive literary skills to fight slavery.

Ottobah Cugoano (c.1757-after 1791)

Quobna Ottobah Cugoano (aka John Stuart) was an enslaved African who wrote and published a passionate biography about his life. He was the first African to publicly call for the abolition of the slave trade and the emancipation of all enslaved Africans. Despite his brief history, there is no detailed account of his capture in Africa, journey across the Atlantic, or experience with slavery in the Caribbean. However, Cugoano as he recounted, was born in a Fante village on the coast of present-day Ghana in 1757. Around the age of thirteen, he was kidnapped outside his village and sold to European slave traders, who carried him across the Atlantic to the southern Caribbean island of Grenada.

Upon arrival, the young Cugoano worked under the evil plantation system and witnessed the most dreadful scenes of misery and cruelty. In fact, while working in the fields with a *slave gang*, he watched other enslaved Africans being severely punished for the most minor offences. After nine to ten months with the slave gang and a year of working in various Caribbean locations owned by his owner Alexander Campbell, Cugoano accompanied him to England in the late 1772. It was while living in England that Cugoano learned to read and write, and also came to believe in Christianity. In June of that year, a few months before Cugoano's arrival, London's Afro-British or black community celebrated the landmark *Somerset* case, which ruled that James Somerset, an enslaved African brought to England by his owner, could not be legally forced to return to the colonies to face chattel slavery. The ruling was won with the help of the abolitionist Granville Sharp, and many black people in Britain viewed it "as a statement of emancipation of slaves in Britain, which [it] was not" (Killingray, 2007). However, the case's success had a considerable impact on progress toward abolition, attracting the British public's attention to the injustices of the slave trade and slavery. Cugoano and Granville Sharp will later cross paths in a similar case.

It is unclear how Cugoano gained his freedom. Some argue that he was formally *freed* by his owner, while others believe he simply liberated himself. Cugoano was baptised on August 20th, 1773, at the age of 16 with the Christian name *John Stuart* at St James's Anglican Church, Piccadilly in London. At the time, it was widely assumed that a black person in Britain who converted to Christianity and received baptism was both physically and spiritually free. In addition, adopting a European name and identifying as a Christian was supposed to provide safety in England. However, neither of these were correct. During this time, some whites were concerned that black spiritual equality might lead to unrealistic expectations of political power. By the mid-1780s, Cugoano was already working as a servant for the renowned painters Richard and Maria Cosway in central London. This type of work was relatively common among former enslaved men at the time. Cugoano became involved in London's African/black community, which numbered around 15,000, and made friends with black abolitionists, such as Olaudah Equiano, Ignatius Sancho and William Green. He later became a prominent black figure and community advocate. In 1786, he and others, joined with Granville Sharp to prevent a black servant, Harry Demane, from being forcibly shipped to the Caribbean by his owner.

After the Demane victory, Cugoano published his book, *"Thoughts and Sentiments on the Evil and Wicked Traffic of the Slavery and Commerce of the Human Species,"* while still living with the Cosways. His book was published in 1787 with the help of his friend Olaudah Equiano, the same year that the Committee for Effecting the Abolition of the Slave Trade was founded. The Committee had twelve founding members, nine were Quakers and the other three were Granville Sharp, Thomas Clarkson and William Wilberforce. They raised public awareness by distributing anti-slavery literature and campaigning to end the slave trade. Cugoano had a lot to say in his book, including dismissing the pro-slavery claims that slavery was divinely sanctioned and that enslaved Africans in the Caribbean had a better life than poor Europeans in Europe. He also argued that every man and woman in Britain shared some responsibility for the enslavement and oppression of Africans. Furthermore, he defended the right of enslaved people to revolt, claiming that "the enslavers of men are the servants of the devil," and "it is the duty of every man to deliver himself from rogues and villains if he can" (Cugoano, 1999). To emphasise the gravity of his opinion, he sent copies of his book to King George III, the Prince of Wales, Edmund Burke, an influential conservative politician and other politicians. There was no proof that any of these people read his book or allowed it to influence their thoughts. It was clear that the royal family was strongly opposed to ending the slave trade.

Following the American Revolutionary War (1775-1783), many blacks came to Britain with their owners who backed the British crown or arrived on their own after fighting for Britain. As a result, there were many unemployed and impoverished blacks in London in 1786, prompting the formation of a commission to remove them. Olaudah Equiano, Cugoano's close friend, was on the committee. Cugoano supported the committee's plan to send black people to Sierra Leone, although he had doubts about the venture's success. Interestingly, within 20 years of Cugoano's first publication, some of his slavery proposals, such as deploying a fleet of ships to the African coast to stop the slave trade, appear to have been carried out.

Cugoano disappeared from history after publishing a shorter version of his 1787 book, *Thoughts and sentiments on the evil of slavery and other writings*, in 1791. His evangelical Christian beliefs clearly influenced his thoughts and feelings in this book, as he used religious arguments to justify its content. There is no record of how he lived the rest of his life. It is assumed that he died in 1791 or 1792. Ottobah Cugoano was an outspoken critic of the trans-Atlantic slave trade and a *radical* in his day. He advocated for the end of slavery as an institution, while others sought only the abolition of the slave trade. His work had a long-term impact, and his ideas influenced Pan-Africanism as a force of enlightenment and liberation.

Plaque Commemorating Ottobah Cugoano In London

Olaudah Equiano (c.1745-1797)

Olaudah Equiano (pronounced ek-wee-AHN-o), aka Gustavus Vassa, was an enslaved African who gained his freedom and wrote one of history's most incredible and well-structured slave narratives. He claimed to have been born in what is now southeastern Nigeria and belonged to the Igbo tribe. Equiano describes how, when he was about ten years old, kidnappers raided his village and kidnapped both his sister and himself, only to separate them and sell them into slavery. There appears to be no record of what happened to his sister after their separation. However, Equiano was transported across the Atlantic on a British slave ship, first to Barbados and then to Virginia, USA.

After surviving the notorious Middle Passage and landing on the island of Barbados, Equiano was transported to the colony of Virginia, where he was purchased by a farmer to do casual work on a tobacco farm. During the summer of 1754, the farmer sold him to a British Royal Navy officer. Interestingly, little black boys like Equiano served as *accessories* for ship captains and women of easy virtue, such as prostitutes or sexually promiscuous women. The naval officer, who was then captaining a merchant ship, renamed him *Gustavus Vassa* after the 16th-century Swedish king. This was the name (his slave name) that he used to identify himself, and it later appeared "in his baptism, his naval records, marriage certificate and will" (Lovejoy, 2006). Olaudah then accompanied his new owner to England, where he was baptised and taught to read and write. In the spring of 1759, he sailed extensively with his owner and witnessed first-hand the Seven Years' War (1756-1763) between Britain and France over colonial and trading rights. During this time, he observed life at sea and learned valuable navigational skills. When he arrived to England, he was surprised to find out that he had been sold to a ship captain bound for the Caribbean island of Montserrat rather than being given his freedom.

When Equiano arrived in Montserrat, he was once again sold to a Quaker merchant, who would become his final owner. However, while in Montserrat, he witnessed numerous forms of cruelty against other enslaved people and felt bad because he couldn't help them. He had to work at several jobs for three years before he could afford to buy his freedom. In 1766, he paid £40 for his freedom. On becoming free, Equiano used his sailing experience to travel the world. His travels included trips to the Mediterranean, Caribbean and Atlantic, as well as a scientific expedition to the Arctic in 1773. After 20 years as an explorer and merchant, Equiano settled in London, England, and got involved in the abolitionist movement. With his new-found political connections and membership in the *Sons of Africa*, he campaigned tirelessly to end the slave trade and eradicate slavery altogether. The *Sons of Africa* was an abolitionist group founded in 1785. It consisted of several educated Africans who had been freed from slavery, such as Olaudah Equiano, Ottobah Cugoano and other leading members of London's black community. Their impact on black people and English society as a whole was to educate and persuade the public about the evils of the trans-Atlantic slave trade and slavery. Equiano and his group collaborated with several important white abolitionists, including Granville Sharpe, Thomas Clarkson and William Wilberforce in their effort to end the slave trade.

In 1789, while the UK parliament was conducting hearings on the slave trade, Olaudah published his famous two-volume autobiography, *The Interesting Narrative of the Life of Olaudah Equiano, or Gustavus Vassa, the African*, in London. He began by providing detailed accounts of his culture, people, and some of their customs and practices, dispelling the European myth that Africans were simply subhuman heathens with no higher purpose in life. He also discussed being kidnapped from his village, walking for six to seven months before reaching the sea coast, the cruelty of slavery he encountered in the Caribbean and Virginia, and how he eventually gained his freedom. Furthermore, during his extensive travels around Britain between 1789 and 1794, he spoke eloquently about the experiences of enslaved Africans and presented a wealth of evidence to support the abolitionist cause, which led to Britain abolishing the slave trade. Some of his critics attempted to discredit him by questioning the authenticity of his story, particularly the location of his birth. Nonetheless, some renowned scholars have carefully examined Equiano's story for linguistic, geographical and cultural details, concluding that he was born in Africa. In any case, according to Gates, Jr. (2002), as cited in Lovejoy (2006), the interesting narrative "became the prototype of the 19th century slave narrative."

The *Interesting Narrative* was a best seller at the time, with nine editions published between 1789 and 1794. It was published in English, Dutch, German and Russian. Equiano decided to keep all rights to his autobiography, control its production, distribution and sale, and register it with the regulating authority as *Property of Author*, whereas most author's signed up with wholesalers and retailers. His choice to self-publish made him a very wealthy black man in 18th century Britain. Nonetheless, many of his critics were surprised that an African man could write so eloquently, due to their own prejudices. His book remains one of the first published by a black African writer. Olaudah Equiano, a genius, died on March 31, 1797 (aged 52), ten years before the slave trade ended in 1807 and forty years before chattel slavery was abolished in British colonies in 1834. He may not have lived to witness these events but his tremendously successful book helped to expose the atrocities and inhumane treatment that millions of enslaved Africans endured during the over 400-year Atlantic Slave trade. In 2009, Olaudah Equiano was honoured with a memorial plaque at St. Margaret's Church in Westminster Abbey, where he was baptised on February 9, 1759. There are also at least two other commemorative plaques in the Westminster area of London where Equiano had lived and worked.

Mary Prince (c.1788-after 1833)

Mary Prince was the first black woman to write about her life in the UK. The book was a first-hand account of an enslaved person, highlighting the horrors of slavery. Mary was born on October 1, 1788, at Brackish Pond, Bermuda, during a period when slavery was widespread in the British Caribbean colonies and throughout the Americas. Her mother was a household slave, while her father, Prince, was a sawyer belonging to a ship builder. When Mary was a baby, the man who owned her family died, and she and her mother were sold as house slaves. Her new owner gave her as a servant to his granddaughter Betsey, who was about Mary's age. Betsey's mother was

Mary's new owner's daughter and her husband was the captain of a ship that traded between America and the West Indies, so he spent a lot of time at sea. Mary thought he was harsh and selfish, and she was always scared whenever he returned home. Mary's siblings were all born while living with her new owner's family. Mary adored her *mistress*, but financial constraints forced the two to part ways. As a result, when Mary was about twelve years old, she was hired out to a woman who lived five miles away. After the unexpected death of her mistress, Mary returned to the household, and the decision was made to sell her. Mary and her two sisters (Hannah and Dinah) were sold to different buyers a few months later. The sisters never saw each other again. This shows how millions of enslaved families were torn apart.

The couple that purchased Mary were uncaring, cruel and abusive. They regularly beat persons in their possession for the most minor of offences. One example of this torture regime occurred when Mary accidentally broke a large cracked clay jar. She was severely flogged by her new mistress, while her husband punched her repeatedly before flogging her 100 times. This was the most frequent form of physical punishment on plantations, and it usually resulted in the skin breaking into tiny strips and leaving permanent marks. Mary also witnessed some of her owners' worst mistreatment of those under their care, including young children. In one extreme case, she witnessed an enslaved woman named Hetty being viciously beaten with a cow-skin. This, combined with multiple blows and beatings, led to the termination of her pregnancy, and eventually, her death. The unchecked brutality and savagery forced Mary to flee to her mother, who had no choice except to hide her in a cave near her home. Mary's father eventually returned her to the custody of her owner. After another five years of maltreatment, Mary was transferred to Grand Turk Island, which was then a Bermuda satellite colony but is now part of the British Crown colony of Turks and Caicos. She was not allowed to say goodbye to any of her family members on the day she left. When Mary arrived on the shores of Grand Turk Island, she was taken to her new owner's home, who had already purchased her from her previous owner. He, like the others, was cold-heartedly cruel, forcing Mary and others under his command to work on his salt ponds for ten years without proper safety equipment. Mary had little choice but to accompany him to his retirement home in Bermuda. Her new job was tedious, but nothing compared to her experience on Turk's Island.

Mary was subjected to further mistreatment and brutality in Bermuda, and one day she found the courage to defend herself by requesting to be placed in the service of another slave owner relocating to Antigua. She was sold for the fifth time between 1816 and 1817 and moved to St. John's, Antigua, with the family of John Adams Wood Jr., where she served as a domestic slave in their home. Mary, aka Molly on the slave register, joined the Moravian congregation in Antigua and learned to read and write there. Shortly after she began to attend the Chapel at Spring Gardens, Mary met Daniel James, a free black carpenter and widower, and they married around Christmas 1826. This angered her owner, who continued to harass and humiliate her before eventually accepting the situation. So, in 1828, at the age of thirty-nine, Mary travelled to London (UK) with her owner and his family, intending to treat her very severe rheumatism and return to her husband as a free woman.

Plaque Commemorating Mary Prince in London

After being mistreated and unable to fulfil the duty assigned to her due to chronic inflammation and pain in her limbs, Mary fled to the Moravian Mission in Hatton Garden (now Holborn). She was subsequently taken to the London Anti-Slavery Society's office, where she was given financial assistance in order to obtain her freedom and write her story. Mary's book, *The History of Mary Prince, a West Indian Slave, Related by Herself,* was published in 1831 and quickly influenced public opinion, contributing to the debate over the abolition of slavery in the British parliament. Her legacy, like that of many other enslaved Africans, was marked by resilience, hope and an unwavering desire for freedom. Mary Prince's memory was honoured in October 2007 with a commemorative plaque placed near her former home in England. Furthermore, her contributions to the abolitionist cause through her sensational life story are widely recognised, and Bermuda declared a public holiday in her honour in 2020. Mary's story also forms part of the permanent exhibition *London, Sugar and Slavery* at the Museum of London Docklands.

Sojourner Truth (1797-1883)

Sojourner Truth (birth name: Isabelle Baumfree) was born into slavery around 1797. She was the youngest of ten or twelve children born to James and Elizabeth Baumfree. Her enslaved family was forced to live in a small, drafty one-room cellar beneath her owner's hotel-style home. The house was in a predominantly Dutch-speaking community in Swartekill, Ulster County, New York. Despite growing up speaking Dutch, the young Sojourner never learned to read or write. Her earliest childhood memories were of hardship and deprivation. However, her Christian faith kept her sane and gave her hope for a brighter future. The majority of what is known about Sojourner comes from her autobiography and transcripts of her various speeches.

Under the chattel slavery, an enslaved person's potential was severely limited in a system that was incredibly cruel and deadly. This instilled a sense of hopelessness and dependency in many enslaved people, and their intellect was crushed. Sojourner began working alongside her mother at the age of five, where she learned vital housekeeping skills. When she was nine years old, her owner, Charles Ardinburgh, died, and she was sold to a farmer for $100, along with a flock of sheep. Her new owner and his wife were extremely cruel to her. Because of their abuse, she sustained severe injuries and was eventually sold to an innkeeper for $105 before being resold to John Dumont, a wealthy farmer, for $70 in 1810 due to financial difficulties. At this time in her life, most of her siblings had been sold. Sojourner worked hard, and Dumont was very impressed by the quality of her work. In 1817, Dumont forced the young Sojourner to *marry* an older enslaved man, with whom she had four children. The marriage was illegal because the civil law did not recognise marriages between enslaved people. Prior to having her four children, Sojourner had a daughter with a fellow slave in 1815, but she was not permitted to marry him. Though slavery in the state of New York was scheduled to end on July 4th, 1827, Dumont broke his promise to free her the previous year. This betrayal annoyed Sojourner, especially since she had worked so hard in preparation for her freedom. This incident influenced her decision to flee with her young daughter, Sophia.

During her escape from slavery in 1826, Sojourner sought refuge and safety with the Van Wageners, a Dutch Quaker/abolitionist family who paid her owner $20 for her labour for the rest of the year. While staying with the Van Wageners, she discovered that Mr Dumont had illegally sold her five-year-old son out of state, and they assisted her in returning him home. Sojourner moved to New York City (NYC) in 1828 for better job opportunities. With the help of a friend, she found steady work as a domestic servant and became involved in church activities. Moving to NYC allowed her to meet several Black community leaders and obtain a better understanding of the abolitionist struggle. By 1843, Sojourner's stay in NYC had become discouraging due to the presence of slave catchers looking for escaped Southern slaves. This dispels the myth that the *North* was a safe haven for enslaved people, as law enforcement officials were compelled by the Fugitive Slave Law to assist in the capture of slaves. Moreover, "New York had the largest slave system of the northern United States" (Somerville, 1994). Only Charleston, South Carolina appears to have matched New York in terms of the extent to which slavery penetrated everyday life.

Additionally, the competition for jobs between blacks and newly arrived European immigrants made life difficult for former enslaved people. On June 1, 1843, Sojourner left NYC to become a travelling preacher. During her travels through the Northeastern United States, she decided to adopt the name Sojourner Truth and started preaching and advocating for black empowerment and women's rights. Her new name had religious connotations because she wanted to highlight her role as a sojourner who guides others to the truth. In 1844, Sojourner joined the Northampton Association of Education and Industry in Massachusetts, which enabled her to travel across the country and speak at anti-slavery rallies. This radically changed her life and gave her the opportunity to meet notable abolitionists like Frederick Douglass, William Lloyd Garrison, Olive Gilbert and David Ruggles at these gatherings.

In 1850, Sojourner's autobiography *"The Narrative of Sojourner Truth: A Northern Slave"* was written by Olive Gilbert and published privately by William Lloyd Garrison. A year later, Sojourner delivered her most famous speech at the Ohio Women's Rights Convention, which included the iconic phrase, "Ain't I a Woman?" Sojourner was invited to meet President Lincoln in October 1864 and was able to tell her story. After her active service in the American Civil War (1861-65), she continued to speak and lecture before retiring to Battle Creek, Michigan, where she died in 1883. Sojourner Truth will be remembered as an abolitionist and women's rights activist. Her legacy is built on the principle of fighting for what is right and honourable.

Frederick Douglass (1818-1895)

Frederick Douglass was a key figure in the abolitionist movement, working tirelessly to end slavery. He was born an enslaved person in Talbot County, Maryland, USA, and given the name Frederick Augustus Washington Bailey. Although his birth date was not recorded, Douglass believed he was born in February 1818 and celebrated it on

February 14. Like so many children of enslaved people at the time, Douglass was separated from his mother, Harriet Bailey, at an early age. It is considered that the practice of taking a new born child from his or her mother was intended to break any natural bond between the two. Douglass rarely saw his mother, who lived on a plantation 12 miles from his home. Sadly, his mother died when he was about seven years old. However, because he had never experienced a mother's love and care, his emotional reaction to her death was similar to that of a stranger. His father was a white man, most likely the slave owner of his family (Captain Anthony). It is commonly known that slave owners frequently raped their female slaves and used the resulting children to increase the slave population and ultimately, their wealth. Douglass was raised on the outskirts of the plantation by his maternal grandmother until the age of six. She also cared for the children of the younger enslaved women. After that, he was moved to another plantation before being sent to Baltimore two years later to look after a couple's young son. Douglass' life was unsettling at such a young age, and he had already faced great hardship and suffering.

Douglass' first experience with reading came when his new owner's wife decided to teach him how to read the alphabets and spell a few basic words. However, as her husband discovered it, he immediately put an end to it, telling her that "learning would *spoil* the best nigger in the world…it would forever unfit him [or her] to be a slave." He also said that enslaved people would "become unmanageable, and of no value to his [or her] master [enslaver]" (Douglass, 1845). These words sank deeply into Douglass' heart and created an entirely new way of thinking, particularly concerning how white men deliberately use these tactics to keep black people ignorant and in control. Nonetheless, he continued to study secretly with the help of some young white boys he met on the streets, eventually learning to read and write. As he read, he became more aware of what had happened to his people and resented his enslavers. Douglass realised that religious slave owners were the most cruel, violent and cowardly people he had ever met. Living in Baltimore exposed him to the magnitude of the brutality meted out to enslaved people on rural plantations, as compared to those in the cities, where living conditions appeared to be less harsh.

When the man who owned Douglass' family died, he was summoned back to the plantation where he was born and valued alongside other property, which included his family members, other enslaved people and a variety of animals. He and his family were eventually inherited by his late owner's daughter, which pleased him because her brother was an alcoholic who had already squandered a large portion of his father's wealth. A month later, when he returned to Baltimore, the owner's daughter, who inherited him, had died. Her husband remarried two years after her death, and in March 1832, he moved Douglass from Baltimore to live with him. Unfortunately for Douglass, he and his new wife were unkind and cruel, frequently depriving him and other enslaved people, including his sister and aunty, of enough food. To survive, they turned to begging and stealing from their neighbours.

As a result of repeated disagreements between Douglass and his owner, he was hired out for a year (January-December 1833) to a local farmer known for physically and psychologically abusing enslaved teenagers. During Douglass' first six months of stay, the farmer, a Methodist church leader, repeatedly abused him, leaving him depressed, devastated and suicidal. He felt broken in *body*, *soul* and *spirit*. However, one day, Douglass decided to fight back. Even though, there was no clear winner, the incident reawakened his desire to live and fight for freedom. For the rest of his stay, the farmer did not assault him again. This reminded Douglass of an incident when he was less than eight years old and witnessed his aunt's brutal flogging and the resistance she displayed in the face of extreme abuse. Douglass then recognised an enslaved person's condition and the choice he or she faced: submit or resist, with the latter ending in harsh physical punishment. On the first of January, 1834, Douglass was hired out again to another farmer. He attempted his first escape a year later while living with this person, but it failed, so he was returned to the couple he had previously lived with in Baltimore to learn how to caulk boats.

Following his training as a skilled caulker, Douglass was hired by local shipyards. At this point, he joined Baltimore's Black community and met his future wife, Anna Murray, a free black woman. Frederick Douglass escaped to New York on September 3, 1838, at the age of twenty, using forged documents produced by Murray, but when he arrived, he had nowhere to stay. After a few days of sleeping rough and going hungry, he was fortunate to meet a kind-hearted white man who invited him to his boarding house and advised him to move to New Bedford, Massachusetts, to avoid being kidnapped by slave catchers. During his brief stay in New York, Douglass married Anna Murray, whom he had invited shortly after arriving. Once he had settled in New Bedford, he adopted the surname *Douglass*. After attending an anti-slavery convention in 1841, Douglass joined the American Anti-Slavery Society and travelled extensively to advocate for abolition.

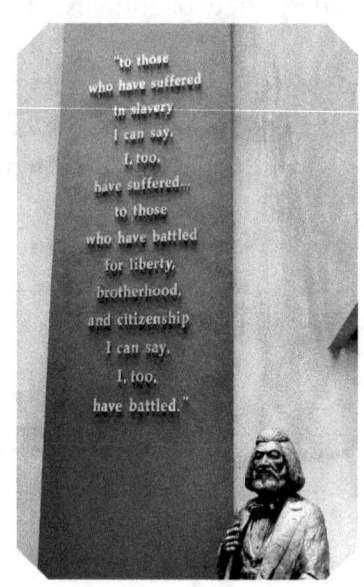

Frederick Douglass National Historical Site

In 1845, he published his autobiography, *"Narrative of the Life of Frederick Douglass, an American Slave [Written by Himself]."* The book was successful, allowing him to travel to the UK and deliver a series of lectures. During his nineteen-month stay in the UK, Frederick's activities and speeches were extensively covered by many prominent British newspapers. In 1846, his supporters (anti-slavery activists) in England helped to buy his freedom, and he returned to the United States as a legally free man.

Frederick Douglass lived a life of courage in the face of adversity. He went from being an enslaved person to becoming an abolitionist, participated in the women's rights movement, started his own newspaper, supported the Union army's war efforts, met with President Lincoln and served in several public positions. In 1852, Douglass was invited to speak in Rochester, New York, and used his speech, *What to the Slave Is the Fourth of July*, to educate people about the evils of slavery and make abolition more acceptable to Northern whites. Frederick Douglass died in 1895, and his story about the evils of slavery influenced public opinion. His legacy as a pioneering abolitionist continues to inspire many people today, and he is widely acknowledged as one of the most influential African American activists in American history, and the father of the civil rights movement.

Harriet Tubman (1822-1913)

Harriet Tubman was popularly known as the *Moses* of her people. She was an enslaved woman of African descent who escaped slavery and chose to help others achieve freedom. Although her actual birth year is unknown, she is thought to have been born around 1820 or 1821 in Maryland's Dorchester County, USA. Other sources, like the US government's 2022 *Harriet Tubman Bicentennial Commemorative Coin Act*, give her birthdate as March 15, 1822. Harriet's parents, Harriet Green and Benjamin Ross, named her Araminta or Minty at birth. She was the fifth out of nine children. While growing up, Harriet was told by older members of the enslaved community that she had the characteristics of an Ashanti/Asante (subgroup of the larger Akan ethnic group) woman, although there is no evidence to support or disprove this assertion.

Harriet was about five years old when she began babysitting her younger siblings and the children of the plantation owner, on whose property her family was enslaved. She was later hired by a cruel couple when she was 6 or 7 years old, and her experience with them left her sick, physically and mentally scarred. Harriet's opposition to slavery and its abuses began around the age of twelve, when she was once again hired as a field hand on a neighbouring plantation. While interfering in an enslaved man's beating, she was accidently hit by a two-pound weight thrown at him by a furious overseer. This resulted in a permanent injury that left her with *narcoleptic seizures* (a tendency to fall asleep) for the rest of her life. Harriet thought slavery was the worst thing ever.

After a partial recovery, Harriet she was hired out for a third time to another plantation owner in 1835 or 1836, where she laboured for 5 to 6 years. Her new location allowed her to be closer to her father while also interacting with free black workers. In this setting, she met her future husband, John Tubman who she married in 1844. At this point, she changed her name from Minty to Harriet. Her marriage was problematic because it involved a free man and an enslaved woman, which created difficulties. Despite this, Harriet persisted, but became concerned when she discovered that she and some of her family members were about to be sold and shipped south.

A similar heartbreaking situation occurred several years ago, when Tubman witnessed the sale of two of her sisters, as was common during slavery. The threat of being sold prompted her to start planning an escape. Harriet believed that escaping would allow her to pursue her lifelong dreams of freedom, equality and justice. One night in 1849, she fled slavery without her husband and followed the North Star to Philadelphia. Harriet's brave escape was remarkable given that the vast majority of runaway enslaved people were men. When she arrived, she got involved in the anti-slavery and Underground Railroad networks, as well as women's suffrage meetings. Through these connections, she found the support she needed to wage a personal war against slavery, and the issues of racial and gender equality that became important to her activism.

The Underground Railroad was a network of anti-slavery activists, safe houses and safe routes. The operation of these networks began in the 1500s and was later linked with the abolitionist activity of the 1800s. These vast and hidden networks facilitated the migration of enslaved people from the South to the North, and eventually, to Canada. The name *Underground Railroad* initially appeared in the early 1830s, coinciding with the introduction of a new rail transit system. Despite the tedious and dangerous journey, Harriet Tubman stayed steadfast, claiming never to have lost a passenger. After making at least thirteen roundtrips into slave-owning states, she was able to personally rescue about 70 enslaved people, including family members and friends. She also taught dozens more how to escape.

Harriet Tubman Commemorative Coin

Harriet's ten-year effort to help enslaved people escape, which began in 1850, elevated her to the status of the Underground Railroad's most famous *conductor*. Her final trip took place in the last quarter of 1860, on the eve of the American Civil War. Also, her love of family and community, combined with her desire to be free, served as significant motivators. Harriet was also a participant in the American Civil War (April 12, 1861-May 26, 1865), functioning as a cook, nurse, armed scout and spy for the Union Army. In fact, she is believed to be the first African-American woman to serve in the military. At the end of the war, she moved to Auburn, New York, and became involved in the women's suffrage campaign. Harriet Tubman was a symbol of courage and freedom. She died in 1913, but her achievements propelled her to the status of a household name, deserving of recognition and commemoration.

> *"The more I read, the more I was led to abhor and detest my enslavers. I could regard them in no other light than a band of successful robbers, who had left their homes, and gone to Africa, and stolen us from our homes, and in a strange land reduced us to slavery. I loathed them as being the meanest as well as the most wicked of men."*
> —FREDERICK DOUGLASS

PORTRAITS OF ENSLAVED NARRATORS

From L-R Top: Olaudah Equiano, Sojourner Truth, Frederick Douglass
From L-R Bottom: Harriet Tubman, Ignatius Sancho

CHAPTER THREE

REBEL LEADERS

Gaspar Yanga (1545-after 1618)

Gaspar Yanga, also spelt Ñanga, was an enslaved African who led a Maroon settlement or *Palenque (pah-LEN-kay)* of enslaved people in the highlands near Veracruz, Mexico (then the Kingdom of New Spain), during the early years of Spanish colonial rule. During the height of chattel slavery in Mexico (1521-1639), the colony had one of the largest enslaved African populations in the Americas. Although Yanga's story has not received the attention it deserves, he was responsible for organising Mexico's most famous rebellion. He is now recognised as one of the first liberators in the Americas, having led one of the earliest slave revolts. In fact, the first recorded large-scale rebellion organised by enslaved Africans in Mexico took place in 1537. Even though the alleged plot did not materialise, it paved the way for enslaved Africans like Yanga and many others to rise up, liberate themselves and challenge colonial authority.

The history of Yanga's childhood was not fully documented. According to local folklore, he was born into royalty around 1545 and was a member of the Bran tribe in present-day Gabon, West Africa. Yanga was also said to have been kidnapped, sold into slavery, renamed, and laboured as an enslaved person. Following the fall of the Mexica (Aztec) Empire in the early 1500s, Spanish colonists began importing an increasing number of enslaved Africans into Mexico. By the 1600s, Mexico had the largest concentration of enslaved Africans in the Americas, and slavery was notoriously brutal. Around 1570, Yanga and a small group of enslaved Africans revolted at a sugarcane plantation near Veracruz, fleeing to a mountainous area that was mostly inaccessible and established a Maroon settlement. Residents felt safe due to their isolation, which attracted other runaways. Yanga and his people survived primarily through farming, though they did occasionally raid Spanish supply convoys.

After nearly 40 years of self-rule, the Spanish colonial government deployed troops in 1609 to destroy the now-extended maroon community and re-enslave Yanga and the other maroons. Yanga and his men, led by Angolan military captain Francisco de la Matosa, defended their settlement with 100 freedom fighters wielding firearms and another 400 armed with bows and arrows, stones, machetes, and other crude weapons. They used their superior knowledge of the area to repel the Spaniards, inflicting heavy casualties and forcing them to negotiate. Yanga sent his terms of peace to end the hostilities, which included requesting a treaty similar to what the indigenous Indians received, meaning an area of self-rule in exchange for tribute and promises to support the Spanish if attacked. To help ease the fears of the region's slave owners, he vowed to return any runaway slaves who entered their proposed territory. Nonetheless, the Spaniards refused the terms and went into battle. After years of fighting, both sides suffered defeats, prompting the Spanish to negotiate with Yanga. The peace treaty was eventually signed in 1618. It granted former enslaved people their freedom and the right to establish their own free settlement. By 1630, Yanga's *Palenque* had evolved into the town of *San Lorenzo de Los Negros*, located in the province of Veracruz. This achievement was unprecedented for its time.

Gaspar Yanga, like many other enslaved Africans who became Maroon figures, represented resistance and freedom for many Africans and their descendants in the Americas and around the world. However, Mexican colonial history attempted to minimise his contributions as being brief and inconsequential in terms of historical significance. In 1860, thirty-one years after Mexico abolished slavery, he was recognised as a Mexican *national hero* and given the title *El*

Primer Libertador de las Americas, or *the first liberator of the Americas*. According to Thompson (2006), "in the 1890s Enrique Herrera Morena, mayor of Córdoba, built a new hospital and named it after Gaspar Yanga…" Yanga is also credited with founding and developing one of the first free towns for liberated Africans in the Americas. In 1932, the town was renamed *Yanga* in his honour. Every year on August 10th, a festival called *El Carnaval de la Negritud* commemorates the legacy of this great African abolitionist, resistance fighter and warrior.

Yanga's monument is prominently displayed in the main square east of Yanga, Veracruz, which is home to one of Mexico's largest Afro-Mexican populations. He would be remembered for organising and leading one of colonial Mexico's first successful slave revolts. On December 7, 2017, a plaque recognising Yanga town as a UNESCO World Heritage Site was unveiled. It honours the memory of slavery and Afro-descendants in the town of Yanga and the state of Veracruz. Approximately, 1.4 million people (citizens) identify as Afro-Mexican or Afro-descendant, accounting for 1.2% of Mexico's population. This was according to a 2015 survey carried out by the Institute of Statistics and Geography (Instituto Nacional de Estadística y Geografía in Spanish). Interestingly, after nearly 500 years in Mexico, Afro-Mexicans, who largely live in states, such as Veracruz, Guerrero, Yucatan, Tabasco, Oaxaca and Baja California Norte, were not recognised as an *ethnic group* until the 2020 census. The results of the most recent census indicated that the overall number of Afro-descendants has increased from 1.4 million in 2015 to 2.6 million in 2020, accounting for 2% of Mexico's population.

Benkos Biohó (late 1500s-1621)

Benkos Biohó (aka Domingo Biohó) was born in the late 1500s on the Bissagos Islands (also spelt Bijagós) off the coast of present-day Guinea-Bissau in West Africa, and was a member of the royal family that once ruled the Islands. The notion that African kings and their families were exempt from being sold into slavery was false; "even kings and other prominent people were enslaved" (Shabaka, 2013). Biohó, a Mandinka by origin, was kidnapped by a Portuguese slave trader and sold to a European slave merchant, who brought him to the Kingdom of New Granada (present-day Colombia) in South America. In 1596, he was sold to a Spaniard in Cartagena de Indias (Cartagena), the 16th century's largest port and slave [human] trafficking market. Many of the early African captives who arrived at the port of Cartagena, like Biohó, were from the Guinea coast (from Guinea-Bissau to central Nigeria). Others eventually followed from the West-Central African coast (from Cameroon to Angola). The cruelty and injustices committed by European slave-owners drove Biohó and around thirty other enslaved Africans (both male and female) to escape from slavery in 1599 or early 1600, after three unsuccessful attempts. The group settled outside of Cartagena de Indias and declared themselves free. Biohó led the settlement or village that they founded, *La Matuna de Palenque*, near the Matuna swamps. To defend their community against Spanish attacks, they formed a guerrilla movement and intelligence network, eventually dominating the Montes de María region on Colombia's Caribbean coast.

Over a five-year period, Biohó and his army conducted many attacks on Spanish authorities from their strategic location. At this point, Biohó was regarded as a great leader, and he declared himself *Rey Del Arcabuco* or *King of the Swamp*. One of Biohó's most clever ideas was to have women use their traditional braided hairstyles (aka cornrows) to convey messages and create escape routes. They also hid gold and seeds in the braids to help them survive once they escaped. After failing to defeat the maroons, the governor of Cartagena presented a peace treaty in July 1605 that essentially acknowledged their territory. As part of the treaty, the community agreed to stop receiving runaway slaves, stop assisting those trying to escape and stop referring to Benkos Biohó as King. However, peace was not achieved until 1612, under the leadership of a new governor. Seven years later, in 1619, the Spanish broke the treaty, conflicts and confrontations persisted, and Biohó was arrested on false charges. On March 16, 1621, Benkos Biohó was publicly hanged, by order of the governor, and his body was mutilated and scattered throughout the city of Cartagena. The governor's motivation for breaking the peace treaty made by his predecessor appears to have originated from his own personal fears, as he saw Biohó as a major threat to his province. Several Palenques were destroyed as a result of the fighting between Spanish forces and maroons, including Biohó's settlement of La Matuna de Palenque.

After Benkos Biohó's death, the insurgency continued and new Palenques were established in the Montes de María region from 1632 onward, including *Palenque de San Miguel Arcángel*, whose emergence was well documented. This demonstrated that killing a man does not mean erasing his ideas. San Miguel and other palenques were attacked by the Spanish authorities in 1694; while most were completely destroyed, San Miguel survived by attracting new groups of runaways from the other destroyed palenques, who rebuilt it into a thriving settlement. A formal peace treaty was reached in December 1713 and signed in January 1714, granting San Miguel Spanish recognition, as directed by the King of Spain. The treaty also granted all escaped enslaved Africans living in San Miguel and the surrounding areas official pardon, autonomy, and the right to live freely on the land. It was later renamed *San Basilio de Palenque*, located in northern Colombia (specifically southeast of the city of Cartagena), which soon became known as *Palenque*, as it still is today.

Several recent studies have challenged Benkos Biohó's claim of founding the town of Palenque, citing a lack of verifiable historical data to support it. However, the studies concluded that "the efforts of Benkos Biohó to seek freedom for slaves started the bases and mechanisms for political negotiations between cimarrones [runaway slaves] and Spanish colonisers" (Camargo and Lawo-Sukam, 2015). According to Navarrete and Herrera (2014), as cited in Guillén (2018), "Palenque de la Matuna is the starting point of a process of marronage in the

Montes de María that concluded with the creation of the town of San Basilio de Palenque [modern-day Palenque]." This may explain why today's Palenque is considered the first free town founded by escaped enslaved Africans in the Americas, as it roots are linked to Biohó's first established Palenque in the early 1600s. Despite its distance from the African coast, the town is marketed as *a proud and independent slice of Africa* in Colombia and Latin America. Its inhabitants, aka *Palenqueros*, are descended from former enslaved Africans who developed a distinct creole language known as *Palenquero*, a combination of Spanish and African Bantu languages (particularly Kikongo), which they alone speak and understand. Palenque remained cut off from Colombia's political, social, and economic landscape for nearly two centuries. The community's isolation and marginalisation from discrimination, racism and ridicule allowed them to preserve traditional practices (social, cultural and spiritual) left behind by their former enslaved African ancestors.

Palenque is today a legendary town with a population of more than 4,000 people, an additional 10,000 within in Colombia's major cities, and a diaspora (outside Columbia) of around 30,000 people who identify as African first and Colombian second. Their African roots serves as the foundation for their rich heritage and culture. The community's social structure, like that of many African societies, is made up of extended family networks, lifetime age groups (kuagros) and councils (juntas) with specific functions. Even funeral rituals have their origins in West Africa. In 2005, the United Nations Educational, Scientific, and Cultural Organisation (UNESCO) recognised their cultural identity and heritage. Today, a statue of Benkos Biohó stands

Statue of Benkos Bioho

prominently in the town to commemorate his liberation struggle and Colombia's long history of black resistance. Biohó's exploits are similar to those of Ganga Zumbi, the leader of Quilombo dos Palmares in Brazil. He is undoubtedly a hero to Colombia's African descendants (aka Afro-descendants), and the heroism and bravery he displayed during his lifetime make him a symbol of the Afro-Colombian Community's current struggle for a decent life, as well as one of the most influential abolitionists in the Americas.

King Cuffy [Cuffee or Kofi] of Barbados (Unknown-Unknown)

Barbados was the second English colony established in the Caribbean, after St Christopher (aka St Kitts), which was regarded to be the *mother colony* of English settlement in the Caribbean. They were set up in 1627 and 1624, respectively. Although many of the planter class belonged to the Church of England, their major objective was not to heighten moral awareness, but rather to protect vested interests. The introduction of sugar to Barbados, the British Empire's main sugar-producing colony, in 1637 triggered an economic revolution that resulted in the mass importation of Africans for forced labour on plantations. According to estimates, 40% of the Africans brought to Barbados between the 1650s and 1710s came from the Gold Coast. Barbados' wealth skyrocketed between 1643 and 1666, with one estimate putting it at forty times its previous level. During the same time period, enslaved Africans who created the wealth through their free labour were treated horribly. The first real threat of a slave revolt in Barbados occurred in 1675, when Cuffy, an enslaved African known as a *Coromantee* (aka Koromantin) or *Gold-Coast* Negro, emerged.

Cuffy is believed to have arrived in Barbados around the middle of the 17th century, and he most likely came from the Akan ethnic group, as did many other early black Barbadians. However, some were taken from West Africa's Upper and Lower Guinea coasts, which include present-day Guinea, Sierra Leone, Liberia, Ivory Coast, Togo, Benin and Nigeria. Despite having complete control of the island, the white minority was always concerned about the growing number of enslaved Africans. As a result, they enacted the Barbados Slave Code in 1661. The extensive law defined Africans as *heathens* and *brutes*, unfit to be governed by the same laws as Christians. It also established standards and procedures for controlling the island's enslaved population, which had tripled since 1640. In fact, the 1661 law was not the first of its kind, but rather a continuation of previous laws, the majority of which limited enslaved Africans' ability to escape or liberate themselves.

Enslaved Africans in Barbados, like others throughout the Americas, desired freedom. During the early years of plantation slavery in Barbados (around the 1640s), many enslaved people wished to escape, and those who did hid in the heavily forested interior, caves and gullies/ravines covered in tropical shrubs and trees, with some individuals occasionally successfully fleeing the island entirely. This was also the time when the majority of the enslaved people were African-born. While a forested interior may seem inconceivable in modern Barbados, forests of huge trees and dense woodlands previously covered the lower slopes to the shoreline before being cleared as sugar plantations expanded. All historical accounts made it clear that the slave code was intended to terrify and scare the enslaved people. However, this did not deter a group of Akan-speaking Coromantee people, who were described by the then-governor of Barbados, Jonathan Atkins, as "a warlike and robust people" (Winkelman, 1976), from plotting to kill their enslavers in 1675 in the hope of gaining their freedom, taking over the island and crowning their leader Cuffy as King of a liberated African state on Barbados.

The impending rebellion, which had been planned for three years, was discovered eight days before its implementation in the summer of 1675 by a female *house slave* who overheard a conversation about it among several enslaved men and told her owner. Those implicated in the conspiracy were quickly arrested and subjected to violent punishments. According to Reid (2013), "107 slaves were accused of involvement and 42 were found guilty and executed publicly [including by hanging and being burned alive], while 5 others hanged themselves because they would not face trial." Following their deaths, the bodies of the suspected ringleaders' were displayed around the streets to serve as a warning to others. The accused plotters were mercilessly executed in Speightstown, the island's second-largest port after Bridgetown, while the enslaved woman who exposed the plot was set free. Although no one knows exactly what happened to Cuffy, he was most likely one of the ringleaders that were executed.

In 1676, a series of laws were passed to protect the island from future insurrections and to restrict the movement of enslaved people. The only other attempts at rebellion by enslaved Africans in Barbados were in 1692 and 1702. Both events were violently suppressed, and those found responsible suffered the same fate as those blamed for the 1675 plot. However, the last and largest rebellion was that of Bussa, which took place in 1816. Although, *Bussa's rebellion* did not go as planned, the insurgent slaves caused financial losses to plantation owners by burning sugarcane fields, resulting in 20% reduction of that year's sugarcane production. The story of *King Cuffy* should be revived and taught in schools as a source of self-determination and pride for all Barbadians and, by extension, the Caribbean.

Ganga Zumbi (1655-1694)

Ganga Zumbi (pronounced: *Zoom-bee*) of Brazil was one of the most famous leaders of Palmares (a name derived from the abundance of palm trees in the region). The autonomous settlement was also called *Angola Janga* [Small Angola] or *Quilombo dos Palmares*, a self-sustaining *quilombo* (a Kimbundu word for war camp) founded in the 1590s after a revolt by enslaved Africans. As a large and diverse Maroon community, it provided a safe haven for Africans fleeing enslavement.

Palmares was an independent confederation of several village-sized *mocambos* (a Kimbundu word for hideout) that stretched two hundred miles long and fifty miles inland from Brazil's northeast coast in Pernambuco, the capital of today's state of Alagoas. By 1640, Palmares had eleven mocambos, each loyal to a specific leader or chief. Quilombo dos Palmares thrived for over a century despite strong opposition from the Dutch and Portuguese colonial authorities.

Zumbi's life began in Palmares, where he was born in 1655. Although nothing is known about his parents, it is presumed that they were from the Kongo province (present-day Angola). Zumbi was about six years old when he was captured by Portuguese soldiers after a failed operation to destroy Palmares. He was taken to a Catholic priest, who baptised him as Francisco. He spent the next several years assisting the priest and learning Portuguese and Latin. Zumbi escaped and returned to his birthplace in 1670, when he was only fifteen. Palmares was described at its peak in 1690, as "an autonomous state, based on African political and religious customs, with between 20,000 and 30,000 [men, women and children] people" (Karasch, 2013). Furthermore, while still in his early twenties, Zumbi was nurtured, raised and developed into a respected military strategist within this free *African kingdom*, led in the mid-1600s by the legendary king Ganga Zumba.

Palmares had a diverse population of escaped Africans, Amerindians, mixed-race ancestry (Caboclos [Amerindian and European] and Mulattos [African and European]), European fugitives or outlaws (pirates and buccaneers), and poor whites, particularly Portuguese military deserters. All elected mocambo chiefs met during times of crisis to discuss critical matters. Such meetings were held at Macaco, Palmares' capital and most populated mocambo, which had about 8,000 inhabitants. Macaco also served as the supreme chieftain's seat. Zumbi will eventually take over this position, succeeding his predecessor, Ganga Zumba. The collective structure of these settlements was complex, but it was often based on African political and religious customs that reflected the diverse ethnicity of its inhabitants. Palmares economy was mainly agricultural however, they also hunted, fished and bred chickens and pigs for meat. Additionally, land ownership was communal, which meant that all property belonged to the entire community. Their religious beliefs and rituals were a mix of Bantu (Central African), indigenous Amerindian and Catholic.

Following the expulsion of the Dutch in 1654, the Portuguese launched a series of military campaigns to destroy Palmares, beginning in the 1670s. The attacks were continuous, but the most serious and destructive occurred between 1675 and 1677, when several mocambos were destroyed. Ganga Zumba was injured during one of these missions, but managed to escape capture. However, in 1678, he accepted a peace treaty brokered by Portuguese officials between planters and maroons, which limited freedom to those born in the mocambos and required Palmares to submit to Portuguese control. This decision was unpopular, and people began to lose confidence in Zumba. The Council of Chiefs eventually chose Zumbi as their new leader and head of the confederation of mocambos. Zumbi pushed for freedom of all enslaved Africans in the Portuguese colonial region. Zumba, on the other hand, left Macaco to form a new settlement near the coast, with up to 400 followers under Portuguese *protection*. In 1680, two years after the treaty was signed, Ganga Zumba died of poisoning, and the sugar planters broke the agreement by re-enslaving many of his followers.

Zumbi became King of Palmares in 1679, ruling from Macaco. He continued to resist Portuguese oppression, adopting a far more militant attitude in the hopes of fighting for Palmares' independence. This commitment boosted his popularity and strengthened his determination to liberate his people. In 1694, almost fifteen years into his reign, the Portuguese authorities assembled a military force of up to 9,000 men to attack Palmares. The expedition's purpose was to conquer Palmares and enslave its people, with the government promising the land of Palmares if they won. The recruited men included prisoners from local jails, whites, Amerindians, mestizos (person of mixed ancestry), and even blacks. The fighting was intense, and after a lengthy and drawn-out battle, the kingdom of Palmares was finally destroyed. Despite surviving the fatal battle, Zumbi and a small group of men fought the Portuguese for over a year before one of his main lieutenants betrayed him after being severely tortured and promised his life and freedom.

Statue of Zumbi Dos Palmares

On November 20, 1695, Zumbi was ambushed, captured and beheaded. To lower the spirits of his people, his body was mutilated, and his decapitated head was publicly displayed to dispel any myths about Zumbi's immortality. The colonial authorities feared what Palmares represented to all enslaved people, so they did everything they could to destroy it, including tracking down and murdering its most famous *Great Chief* or King, Zumbi. Even after Zumbi's death, Palmares survivors continued to revolt, rebel and resist the Portuguese, with many escaping to emerging quilombos during the period of Brazilian slavery. Zumbi was a legendary leader whose name is widely respected throughout Brazil. He was the last warrior-king of Palmares, and many Afro-Brazilians and African descendants regard him as a hero, freedom fighter and symbol of liberty. In 1984, the drama film *Quilombo*, based on the history of Palmares and featuring the exploits of Ganga Zumbi, was released and screened at the Cannes Film Festival. Every year (since 1978), on November 20, Brazil's National Black Consciousness Day, Afro-Brazilians commemorate Ganga Zumbi's life and legacy. He is fondly remembered for his courage, leadership qualities and heroic battles for justice, equality and freedom.

Prince Klaas [Kwaku Takyi] aka King Court (c.1690-1736)

Prince Klaas (aka King Court) is one of Antigua and Barbuda's national heroes. In 1736, he initiated a conspiracy to overthrow white rule on the island of Antigua. Klaas, also known by his African name Kwaku Takyi, was born in Ghana (formerly the Gold Coast) in 1691 and belongs to the Akan ethnic group. He was captured as a child and brought to Antigua in 1701. The young Klaas was one of millions of African captives forced to endure inhumane conditions on slave ships crossing the Atlantic. The African captives aboard these ships were brutalised, intimidated and subjected to daily abuse. In other words, they needed to be physically strong, mentally tough and spiritually sound in order to complete the journey. The death rate among those who arrived safely was extremely high. In Barbados, for example, it was estimated that more than 150,000 enslaved people would be required to maintain a stable population of around 20,000. As an enslaved person, Klaas became the property of a wealthy Antiguan trader who was also a plantation owner, justice of the peace and speaker of the assembly, subjecting him to constant labour and harsh discipline. Despite the stresses and unpredictable nature of the slave system, Klaas' intelligence was recognised by his owner, who elevated him to the position of Head Slave.

While Klaas enjoyed greater privileges than most other enslaved persons on the island, he never forgot his African heritage. With this in mind, he dreamt of freedom for himself and his people. Over an eight year period, Klaas and other enslaved people met at a place called Stone Hill Gully, secretly plotting a rebellion against the island's planters. Prior to Prince Klaas' attempted revolt, Antigua witnessed various acts of anti-slavery resistance. For example, in the 17th century Antigua, when the island was sparsely populated, a number of enslaved Africans (mostly African-born) rebelled against their enslavement and escaped to the wild interior around the summit of

Antigua's extinct volcano, Boggy Peak (aka Mount Obama), where they established maroon villages. In 1687, there was a harrowing episode involving a runaway slave who was recaptured. In that case, after being labelled as rebellious, the offender was found guilty and sentenced to be burned to ashes, while another, who only carried messages, had his leg amputated. This treatment was insufficient to deter others. Antigua's first recorded uprising occurred in 1701, when fifteen recently arrived Coromantee slaves murdered their owner, for refusing to give them a Christmas holiday break. Even after the punitive Slave Act of 1702, followed by another in 1723, resistance persisted, most notably with the planned estate revolt of 1729 and Klaas' 1736 island-wide conspiracy. The former was a failed conspiracy in which three enslaved Africans were burned alive and a fourth hung. The next significant revolt after that of Klaas occurred in 1831, when enslaved Africans protested against the closure of the Sunday market.

Prince Klaas and his fellow conspirators planned to take advantage of King George II's coronation ceremony, which was set to take place in St. John's, the island's capital, in October 1736. The plan was to put a 10-gallon barrel of gunpowder into the building and blow it up. The subsequent explosion was intended to serve as a signal to enslaved people on neighbouring plantations to rise up, leading to the widespread killing of planters and Prince Klaas emerging as the leader of a new black kingdom on the island. Prior to the proposed conspiracy, Klaas allegedly attended a public ceremony where he was crowned *King of the Coromantees*, the Akan-speaking ethnic group to which he belonged, by an obeah-man and declared war on slave owners. While Europeans who witnessed the ceremony dismissed it as mindless entertainment, enslaved Africans recognised the significance of traditional Akan war dance, drumming and rituals such as those performed by an Ashanti king.

Unfortunately, Prince Klaas' vision of freeing his people from slavery was discovered by chance, after the coronation ceremony had been postponed for nearly three weeks, and some enslaved people began to boast that things were about to change. This raised the suspicions of a few white people, prompting a full-scale criminal investigation. Klaas was later arrested, along with his chief lieutenant, Tomboy, and several other conspirators. Many of the detained participants were subjected to severe torture, which provided evidence for their prosecution. In retaliation, Klaas and his followers were found guilty and sentenced to death by using a variety of horrific methods. On October 20th, 1736, Prince Klaas' body was crushed by a wheel. This was a cruel form of crucifixion in which every bone in a person's body was gradually broken, causing them to die slowly from shock or internal bleeding. A total of 132 enslaved people were convicted, with 88 brutally executed. Of these, five (including Klaas), were broken on the wheel, six were hanged from a gibbet (killed over several days) and 77 were burned alive. The horrific, barbaric and brutal executions lasted until March 8, 1737, and were meant to discourage others from committing similar acts in the future.

A monument to Prince Klaas can be found in Antigua and Barbuda's capital, St. John's. The statue honours his resistance and brave attempt to free all enslaved Africans in Antigua. It was erected in 1993 and serves as a reminder of the cruelty and inhumanity of slavery not only in Antigua and Barbuda, but throughout the Caribbean and the Americas. Prince Klaas stands out as an Antiguan national hero, having established a proud tradition of resistance to all types of injustice. His legacy and popularity lives on.

Statue of Prince Klaas

Francois Mackandal (unknown-1758)

Francois Mackandal (also spelt Macandal or Makandal) was a great Haitian revolutionary and maroon leader. He escaped slavery as an adult around 1746, leading one of several uprisings that occurred before the Haitian Revolution. Mackandal was a thorn in the side of the French, and his declaration and certainty that slaves will overthrow the French and abolish slavery makes him the chief architect and progenitor of the Haitian Revolution. He is thought to have been born in the Upper Guinea region of West Africa or the West Central region of Kongo-Angola before being moved to the colony of Saint-Domingue, where he began working on a large sugar plantation around the age of twelve. According to oral history and conventional research, Mackandal was well-educated before his enslavement and could speak and write Arabic fluently. This could explain why some sources identified him as Muslim, leading to suspicion that he was from Senegal, Mali or Guinea. However, due to his extensive knowledge of Vodou and his status as a Vodou high priest, people linked him with this religion instead. As it was throughout slavery, plantation life was harsh and terrifying. This would have sped up Mackandal's escape, especially after he accidentally lost his hand in a sugar mill's grinding machine and was forced to look after cattle. Accidents like these were common in Caribbean sugar mills where enslaved people were made to work shifts of 16-18 hours per day, especially during the harvest and milling season.

After fleeing the plantation, Mackandal joined a maroon group and rose quickly to the position of leader. He evaded capture for many years and was able to unite the various maroon groups that lived in the island's remote mountain regions. From 1751 to 1757, he led raids and attacks against the French, using guerrilla warfare techniques and spiritual beliefs. At the time, the maroons consisted of both escaped enslaved Africans and surviving Amerindian groups, such as the Tainos. These communities formed an effective secret movement thanks to their combined abilities and an underground network of enslaved people recruited from plantations. Lacking the required weapons to fight the French, Mackandal relied on his extensive knowledge of tropical herbs and medicinal plants to make poisons, portions and remedies from local plants. These were distributed to thousands of trusted allies on plantations, who mixed them into the foods and drinks of slave owners and planters and their families. Untrustworthy enslaved individuals who appeared to support whites were also poisoned. Many people were killed before the conspiracy was discovered.

For a long period of time, the white population of Saint-Domingue lived in fear and hysteria, since French officials were unable to determine what was causing their illnesses and deaths. While this was going on, Mackandal was planning a rebellion. *The Mackandal Conspiracy*, as it was known, was a large-scale poisoning plot designed to eliminate white slave owners and planters across Saint-Domingue. He was said to have trained an *army* of skilled poisoners with the objective of poisoning the wells [water supply] in Cap-Francais, aka Le cap (now Cap-Haitien). The plot's success would have led to the overthrow of the French colonial authority and put an end to slavery, but Mackandal was betrayed by an enslaved woman who was tortured after being apprehended. Later, he and some of his followers were caught. According to an anonymous letter, as the conspiracy progressed and before its discovery, "as many as 30-40 whites, including women and children, and about 200-300 other enslaved people and animals were killed in the Mackandal conspiracy" (Eddins, 2022).

On 20th January, 1758, Mackandal was summarily tried and sentenced to be burned alive in Cap-Francais' public square. Thousands of enslaved people from hundreds of plantations were forced to travel from across the colony to witness his brutal torture and death. Despite seeing him being burned alive, many in attendance felt that his soul had escaped the flames, meaning that he was still alive and would return to fulfil his prophesies. This incident, combined with his prophesy about the ultimate freedom and independence of the enslaved black population, cemented his reputation as a legendary and inspirational figure throughout the Haitian revolution. Moreover, some historians believe his intended revolt marked the start of the Haitian revolution. As a result, Mackandal has become one of Haiti's national heroes, and his legacy is preserved in Haitian folklore, telling the story of a powerful, brilliant, charismatic and well-organised maroon leader. Even though the historical accuracy of Mackandal's life has been called into question, his role as a rebel leader in the fight for Haitian independence has been immortalised in the minds of Haitians, with his image embossed on a commemorative Haiti twenty Gourdes gold coin issued in 1967.

Nanny of the Maroons (c.1686-c.1760)

Nanny of the Maroons was a legendary female freedom fighter in the New World. She was a prominent leader among Jamaica's Windward Maroons, a community of former enslaved Africans living on the island's eastern region. Queen Nanny (aka Granny Nanny) is an iconic figure in Jamaican history. Her life story is based on oral history from Jamaica and some British records. Nonetheless, it is widely accepted that Nanny was born around 1686 on the Gold Coast (present-day Ghana) of West Africa and belonged to the Ashanti tribe. Besides, there are conflicting accounts of how she came to Jamaica. Some sources claim she arrived as a free woman, while others believe she arrived as an enslaved person. What is certain, however, is that she and a group of other enslaved people ran away from the brutality of the British slave system to Jamaica's Blue Mountains, where they established a Maroon community. Even before Nanny and her group's *grand marronage* (escape from the plantation with no intention of ever returning), other enslaved African groups had taken the same path to freedom since the British invasion of Jamaica in 1655. The desire to escape to freedom was mostly driven by newly arrived

Africans who had not completed the two to three-year *seasoning* period of working on plantations. During a speech to the British Parliament in 1789, in an attempt to persuade his colleagues to end the slave trade, William Wilberforce stated unequivocally that "a third [33.3%] of slaves die during the seasoning period" (Carey, 2003). This clearly shows the brutality of the process (physical and psychological torture), but the slave trade continued for another 18 years.

Nanny is described as having exceptional leadership qualities, and her influence over the Maroons was enormous. She was also regarded as a great *obeah* (a term used to describe folk magic and religion with West African influences) woman who used her supernatural abilities to protect her warriors against their British adversaries. By 1720, Nanny was leading and controlling the Windward Maroon settlement of Nanny Town. The settlement is said to have resembled a typical African village, providing a safe haven from British enslavers who threatened to recapture or kill them. During the First Maroon War (1728-1739), Nanny and her warriors used guerilla warfare tactics to inflict greater losses on the British, who were frequently ill-equipped and unprepared to fight in such hostile terrain. As a military strategist, she taught maroon fighters how to disguise themselves with branches and leaves to look like trees. When they spotted the enemy, they would quickly surround and capture them. Nanny's military experience enabled her to organise and execute successful maroon raids. She is credited with freeing more than 1,000 enslaved Africans from slavery.

In addition, Nanny's supernatural powers and Obeah practice were credited with the maroons' successful resistance to British attacks. Obeah, in particular, was used to protect and instill confidence in the maroon fighters. When the British realised they couldn't defeat the Maroons militarily, they were forced to negotiate a peace treaty with the island's two main Maroon groups: Windward (inhabited the eastern part of Jamaica) and Leeward Maroons (occupied the western part). The latter were led by Captain Kojo (also spelt Cudjoe) and

Accompong (also spelt Akropong), both known as Nanny's *brothers*. Kojo signed the Leeward Maroons treaty in 1738, and the Windward Maroons followed suit in 1739. The maroons were unaware that these treaties represented the first steps toward their integration into Jamaican society. However, they viewed it as an acknowledgment of their independence. Nonetheless, as autonomous groups, Jamaican maroons were widely recognized as a slave society with a history of rebellions and successes. Their primary goal was to protect their own sovereignty.

Surprisingly, Nanny was not the Windward Maroon representative that signed the Treaty with the British. It was actually signed by Captain Quao, another powerful Windward Maroon leader. According to oral history, Nanny refused to sign the treaty because she was upset and opposed to the principle of peace with the British, fearing that it would lead to further suppression. Prior to the signing of the peace treaties, the British destroyed Nanny Town, a Windward Maroon stronghold, in 1734 after a series of attacks that claimed many lives. Rather than give up, Nanny and her remaining followers sought refuge and regrouped in Guy's Town, a nearby Maroon settlement. In 1740, the Windward Maroons were granted 500 acres of land, as a result of the 1739 treaty. This resulted in the establishment of New Nanny Town in the Parish of Portland. Following Nanny's request, the Windward Maroons were later granted additional land, and the town was renamed Moore Town. It is worth noting that there are "four widely recognised Maroon communities in Jamaica: Accompong [Town], Charles Town, Moore Town and Scott's Hall" (Connell, 2017). These four towns are descended from the historical Leeward and Windward Maroon groups, respectively.

Although the exact year of Nanny's death is unknown, most people believe she died of natural causes sometime in the 1760s. Nanny lived her life guided by her African ancestors' spiritual beliefs, and she collaborated with other Maroons to preserve their African culture and tradition. Despite the fact that Nanny did not have her own children,

Bump Grave - Nanny of The Maroon's Resting Place

all Maroon consider themselves as *Nanny Pikibo*, or Nanny's children. In 1975, the Jamaican government declared Queen Mother Nanny a National Hero and erected a monument in her honour. On March 31, 1982, she received the Order of the National Hero, with Sam Sharpe, the leader of the Baptist War of 1831-1832. This means that they, like other Jamaican national heroes, should be referred to as "The Right Excellent." Nanny is recognised as the most significant female rebel leader in Jamaican history, as well as a symbol of Jamaican nationalism. Her portrait is on the old Jamaican $500 banknote, which has been replaced with an upgraded version of the same denomination featuring Nanny and Samuel Sharpe together. Nanny of the Maroon was a brave leader, military strategist and an important spiritual figure who used guerilla warfare to effectively fight oppression. Her legacy shows that women can achieve the highest levels of leadership in any society.

Bokilifu Boni (1730-1793)

Bokilifu Boni was a Maroon leader who led an armed rebellion against Dutch oppression and dominance in Suriname. His influence was so strong that his people became known as the Boni people (later the Aluku). Boni was born in a jungle near the Cottica River in Suriname around 1730, after his enslaved African mother (whose name was unknown) escaped the plantation while heavily pregnant. At this time, Suriname was then under Dutch colonial rule, and slavery was a barbaric practice. The brutality of the slave system was documented in the personal diary and narrative (first published in 1796) of Captain

REBEL LEADERS

John Gabriel Stedman, a Scottish-Dutch soldier and anti-Maroon mercenary who was one of almost 1600 men brought in to put down slave revolts in Suriname.

Boni was of mixed ancestry (creole), as his father was a white man (most likely Dutch) who may have used his mother as a concubine or been a victim of sexual abuse. The latter was a regular occurrence during slavery, with many enslaved African girls, women and occasionally men, being routinely raped by their owners. This act of violence had no consequences because an enslaved person had no legal rights. The vast majority of children born as a result of such interactions were considered as slaves and unable to integrate into white society. Boni grew up in the forest with the Cottica Maroons, as they were originally known, and learnt a variety of skills, including hunting and fishing. By 1760, Boni and his people had settled along the Cottica River. They were led by Asikan Sulvester, who escaped from a plantation in 1712, shortly after arriving from Africa. An aging Sulvester will later pass on his authority to two successors, Boni and Aluku.

Around 1765, Boni became the tribe's leader, sharing power with the elder, Aluku. He was in charge of protecting his people militarily, while the elder looked after the women and children. Boni tried from the start to negotiate a peace treaty with the Dutch authorities, as did two other Maroon groups, the Ndyuka and the Saamaka (aka Saramaka), who were successful in 1760 and 1762, respectively. The latter is regarded as the first organised Maroon group, having formed in the late 17th century. Interestingly, these treaties with both groups, which are similar to those signed with several other maroon groups across the Americas (including Jamaican maroons), granting them the right to occupy their land and recognising them "as free, with autonomy in their social, political and land management" (Bellardie and Heemskerk, 2019). Other major clauses of the treaties required maroon groups to hand over any new escaped slaves seeking refuge in their territory, as well as to keep a colonial government representative living among them. This person was in charge of keeping daily records of activities and reporting them to the Dutch authorities. However, Boni's request for a peace treaty was denied by the Society of Surinam[e], a private management company established to oversee the colony of Surinam[e]. Instead, they started a war with the Aluku Maroons.

After discovering and destroying their main village in 1768, Boni and his warriors decided to construct a large and heavily guarded fortress in a swamp, which they named Fort Boekoe. This was the beginning of first Boni War, which lasted from 1768 to 1776. As the tribe grew in size, especially after being joined by two smaller Maroon groups, the Alukus launched well-organised attacks on plantations around the Cottica River and east of Suriname. Fortunately for them, their swampy location was fortified with five-meter-high walls and cannons to deter potential attacks. Due to Boni's numerous successes in raiding plantations, some enslaved people escaped and joined him. As a result, the planters became concerned about the loss of slaves (which represented a large loss of wealth), and they were determined to discover and destroy their impenetrable fortress.

Between 1772 and 1775, Boni intensified his efforts to defend his stronghold by raiding plantations for supplies on a regular basis and increasing the number of runaway slaves. Since the colony's army was unable to defeat Boni and his men, Suriname's Governor General, Jan Nepveu, formed a Black Soldiers Corps (aka *Redi Musu* or *Black Rangers*). This group of 300 former enslaved people, purchased by the colonial government from plantation owners, successfully penetrated and destroyed the fort in August 1775. According to Stedman's account, "the [black] Rangers [were] much better adapted to forest fighting... [and] were competent in guerilla warfare... one [black] Ranger is worth six European soldiers" (White, 2001). After the fort was destroyed, Boni and his group fled east for refuge and in 1776, crossing the Maroni or Marowijne River (which serves as the border between French Guiana and Suriname) and settled on the French banks. The migration brought them into close proximity to

Ndyuka-Maroon territory, prompting clashes until an uneasy truce was reached in 1779. This resulted in both groups creating a bond, which was strengthened by marital relations and regular blood oath ceremonies.

The colonial authorities frowned on this alliance and threatened to break the treaty it had signed with the Ndyukas. However, because they were intent to eradicate a far more militant Aluku, hostilities with the Dutch resumed, resulting in the Second Boni War (1789-93). Following the Dutch/Ndyuka treaty and the development of a new generation of leaders, the Ndyuka-Maroons separated from the Aluku and joined forces with the colonists. Hostilities with the Ndyuka worsened, and in February 1793, Boni was betrayed and murdered by Bambi, an Ndyuka leader and colonial government ally. The majority of Aluku Maroons were forced to relocate upstream of the Maroni River, where they later signed a treaty with the French authorities in 1860. Marronage did not end in Suriname with Boni's death, but continued on a smaller scale until slavery was abolished in 1863. Boni is a legendary figure among the Aluku and other Maroon communities of Suriname and French Guiana, and his legacy continues to inspire.

Gabriel Prosser (1776-1800)

Gabriel Prosser was a literate enslaved blacksmith who had grown tired of being owned by others. He is best remembered for planning what would have been the largest slave revolt in US history. His uprising encouraged subsequent generations of enslaved rebels. Gabriel was born as an enslaved person in 1776 on a tobacco plantation in Henrico County near Richmond, Virginia. Although nothing is known about his parents, records show that he had two brothers, Solomon and Martin. Gabriel learnt to read at a young age and was among the South's only 5% literate enslaved people. By the age of 20, he was well over six feet tall, and his physical stature, along with his literacy skills and fighting ability, made him an ideal leader. In 1798, Gabriel's owner died and his 22-year-old son inherited him along with the other enslaved people. As was typical for slave owners with skilled slaves, Gabriel's services as a blacksmith were hired out, allowing him to travel freely to work around Henrico County and Richmond. However, he was only permitted to keep a small portion of his earnings, with the rest going to his owner.

According to some historians, an incident in 1799 influenced Gabriel's decision to plan a rebellion. The incident happened after Gabriel got into a fight and injured (bit a portion of the man's left ear) a neighbouring white overseer who accused Jupiter, an enslaved man, of stealing a pig and Solomon, Gabriel's brother, of threatening him. Gabriel's reaction was seen as excessive and a crime. Fortunately for him, he received a lighter sentence and was not executed, which would have been the appropriate punishment for such an act. The justices who presided over the trial found Jupiter guilty but Solomon not guilty. Gabriel was sentenced to one-month in jail and had his left thumb publicly branded (burnt). The sentence reflected his valuable skill as a trained blacksmith, which was financially beneficial to his owner. After this experience, Gabriel's determination to resist slavery grew stronger. During this time, he married his wife, Nanny.

Gabriel began plotting his uprising in the spring of 1800, informing those closest to him. Other factors that influenced his decision included the rhetoric of the American Revolution (i.e. *the right to be free, all men are created equal, unalienable rights given to all humans by their creator - life, liberty and the pursuit of happiness*); the uprising that led to the Haitian Revolution; his own hatred for the system of slavery that brutalised him and other enslaved people; the perceived success of free blacks; and his desire to be free and prosper. His new disciples, including his brother Solomon, began recruiting not just in Henrico County, but also in Richmond and other towns and counties around Virginia. They would typically ask prospective recruits if they wanted to join and fight for their freedom. As people joined the planned insurrection, word spread quickly through the port town's back alleys, hidden taverns, warehouses and docks. Essentially, they were preparing for what would become the largest slave revolt in US history.

In preparation for the revolt, they began collecting weapons by altering agricultural hand tools into swords and ammunition. Gabriel and over 1,000 men were ready to unleash mayhem on their enslavers by August 1800, and they planned to do it on the night of August 30. The original strike date was pushed back due to a rainstorm and rescheduled for the following night, as fast rising water rendered major roads and bridges impassable. Before they could launch the attack, Gabriel was betrayed by some fearful enslaved people, as was common in slave rebellions. The first conspirators' trials and executions started in September. One strategy for persuading enslaved people to reveal the identities of conspirators was to grant full pardon to a handful of them. Gabriel was captured and tried after evading authorities for several weeks with a $300 bounty on his head. He refused to testify, and by the end of October, more than two dozen alleged rebels had been executed. Gabriel was instantly hanged on October 10, 1800. Many suspects arrested in neighbouring counties experienced similar outcomes. Even though Gabriel's insurrection did not succeed, it's meticulous planning terrified white enslavers and showed that some enslaved people would go to any length to achieve freedom.

Following the insurrection, the state compensated Virginia slave owners for the loss of property (i.e. enslaved people) totalling more than US$9000 (about US$200,000.00 today). Furthermore, as was customary whenever there was a revolt or threat of a revolt, the authorities enacted new harsh laws to restrict the movement of enslaved people and free blacks across Virginia and beyond. However, on the 202nd Anniversary (in 2002) of Gabriel's planned revolt, the City of Richmond passed a resolution in his honour. In 2007, Virginia's Governor informally pardoned Gabriel and his co-conspirators, acknowledging that his cause to end slavery and promote equality for all people had been successful in the eyes of history. Gabriel's uprising has received countless praises in recent decades, but descendants of enslaved people have yet to receive any form of reparations.

Toussaint L'Ouverture (1743-1803)

Toussaint L'Ouverture was a key figure in the slave revolt on French-controlled Saint-Domingue, which triggered the Haitian Revolution (1791-1804). However, he followed in the footsteps of Jamaican-born and grand Vodou priest Dutty Boukman (aka Bookman), the fearless leader who sparked the August 1791 uprising that eventually led to the Haitian revolution. Before being killed by the French in November 1791, Boukman urged the enslaved population to reject the image of the oppressors' God and predicted that the revolt would free the enslaved people of Saint-Domingue. The success of the revolution, which established the first Black Republic in the Western Hemisphere, fuelled the belief that slavery could be abolished across the Americas. Although little is known about Toussaint's early life, he was born a slave around 1743 and given the name François Dominique Toussaint. His father, Gaou-Guinou, is thought to be the son of a king from the Arrada (also spelt Allada) kingdom in what is now the Republic of Benin who was kidnapped by slave traffickers on the African coast and sold into slavery in Saint-Dominque, a French colony on the island of Hispaniola (now the Dominican Republic and Haiti). Toussaint was the oldest of eight children, brought up in a tough and violent environment for enslaved Africans. He was fortunate as a child to have learned to read and write. Toussaint's intelligence and hard work were recognised, and he was set free in 1776.

Before the Haitian revolution, Toussaint had married an enslaved woman named Suzanne Simon-Baptiste and was managing the workforce on his former owner's plantation. He joined the rebellion as the enslaved population revolted on August 22, 1791, burning down plantation houses and farms. Toussaint quickly established himself as a capable soldier, climbing through the ranks to become one of the revolution's key figures. He eventually added *L'Ouverture* (French for opening) to his name, most likely to reflect his ability to open gaps in enemy lines. During the struggle for independence, Toussaint led thousands of well-organised enslaved Africans into battle against French, Spanish and British forces. Not surprisingly, the rebellion stirred up colonial ambitions among competing European powers, who saw it as an opportunity to drive France out of its richest colony, which was by far the Caribbean's wealthiest and most prosperous slave colony. Historians estimate that in the 1780s, Saint-Domingue accounted for up to 40% of France's foreign trade and supplied half of Europe with cotton, sugar and coffee. By 1789, Saint-Domingue had more than 7,000 thousand plantations of which 3,000 produced indigo, 2,500 coffee, 800 cotton and about 50 cocoa. However, sugar was the backbone of her economy and the key to her rapid growth. Because the French were already losing ground to the Spanish and their British allies, with whom they declared war in 1793, they decided to offer freedom to all rebel slaves, hoping to encourage them to switch sides in the battle. On February 4th, 1794, the French officially abolished slavery in their colonies. Toussaint and his army, now free, fought for the France, reversing the British victories and expelling the Spaniards from Santo Domingo (present-day Dominican Republic), in eastern Hispaniola.

With slavery abolished in Saint-Domingue, Toussaint L'Ouverture emerged as the undisputed revolutionary leader from 1794 until 1801. In July 1801, he issued his Constitution, which abolished slavery in Santo Domingo, removed racial privileges, and reaffirmed the legitimacy of the newly emancipated colonies. This elevated him to the rank of General-in-chief, overseeing the entire island of Hispaniola. During his term, Toussaint declared that all people of the unified island were legally equal, regardless of colour, race, or condition. He worked tirelessly to improve the economy by establishing free trade while also continuing to protect the island. Unfortunately,

Toussaint Louverture
(1743 - 1803)

Héros de la lutte pour l'abolition de l'esclavage et précurseur de l'indépendance d'Haïti

Statue of Toussaint L'Ouverture - Hero of the fight for the abolition of slavery and precursor of Haitian independence

Toussaint's government would face difficulties with the rise of Napoleon Bonaparte. In May 1802, Bonaparte reinstated slavery in the French Caribbean colonies, with the exception of Guadeloupe, Guyane and Saint-Domingue, and ordered that the slave trade adhere to pre-1789 laws and regulations. Nonetheless, France was eager to recolonise Saint-Domingue and sent a military invasion force of about 20,000 troops, led by General Leclerc, Napoleon's brother-in-law, to retake control. During the invasion, the French seized the Spanish-speaking part of the island and immediately reintroduce slavery. However, after numerous failed attempts to destabilise and seize control of Saint-Domingue, General Leclerc invited Toussaint under false pretences and proposed negotiating a peace treaty. When Toussaint arrived for the meeting, he was arrested on false allegations.

Following his arrest, Toussaint warned his captors that the rebels would not retreat, saying, "In overthrowing me, they have uprooted in Saint-Domingue only the trunk of the tree of the liberty of the blacks; it will grow back because its roots are deep and numerous" (Jenson, 2010). He was then taken to France and imprisoned in a cold, damp and dark cell from January 1803 until his death on April 7, 1803. Toussaint died from pneumonia and malnutrition. Despite receiving written reports from the prison guard about his deteriorating health, the French authorities did not send a doctor to examine him. The success of the Haitian revolution was accomplished on January 1, 1804, under the leadership of Jean-Jacques Dessalines. Toussaint's words came back to haunt France. Toussaint L'Ouverture, known as the Black Napoleon in some circles, was a true political genius and a statesman. His courageous actions shocked the institution of slavery and popularised the idea of freedom for black people and all oppressed people in the Americas.

Jean-Jacques Dessalines (1758-1806)

Jean-Jacques Dessalines led the Haitian revolution, which was victorious in January 1804. He was the general who succeeded Toussaint L'Ouverture, defeated Napoleon's army and declared Haitian independence after removing French rule. According to Haitian legend, Dessalines was born in Africa, most likely in the ancient Kingdom of Kongo (present-day northern Angola and the Republic of Congo), then enslaved in Saint-Domingue, France's richest colony. Most historians, however, believe he was born in 1758 on the island of Saint-Domingue to Congolese parents under the name Jean-Jacques Duclos. His surname, like that of other enslaved people at the time, came from the plantation owner who had enslaved his parents when he was born.

The slave system in Saint-Domingue was notoriously brutal, with various forms of torture, extreme and sadistic punishments (mutilation and burning) and sexual abuse. As was common on most plantations, parents like Dessalines were sold to neighbouring plantations, and their children were cared for by older enslaved women. Dessalines is said to have been watched over by a woman believed to be one of Dahomey's legendary Amazons. She taught him the skills of an African warrior that he could use in his future endeavours. The young Dessalines experienced the horrors of slavery and was denied the opportunity to learn to read and write. Nevertheless, he rose from farm hand to foreman. When Dessalines reached the age of 30, he was purchased by a free black landowner and adopted the owner's surname, *Des Salines*. The cruelty and violence of slavery drove him to escape in 1791 and join the revolution. Dessalines fighting and leadership abilities propelled him to the rank of lieutenant in the revolutionary Army. After meeting Toussaint L'Ouverture (the revolution's main general) and proving himself, Dessalines was promoted to second-in-command and given the nickname *Tiger* for his fury and bravery in battle. Throughout the insurgency, Dessalines used his exceptional military abilities to defeat his opponents. His tactics were swift and brutal, and he was known for not sparing any prisoners. Many people believe his brutality was motivated by his observations and experiences on the plantations.

Following Toussaint L'Ouverture arrest and deportation to France, Dessalines took charge of the Saint-Domingue liberation forces and resumed the war against the French. With the support of Toussaint's lieutenant, Henry Christophe, as well as several black revolutionaries and other mulatto leaders like Alexandre Pétion, the French were eventually defeated in November 1803. After thirteen years (1791-1804) of fighting, enslaved Africans liberated themselves, abolished slavery on the island, and overcame French colonists as well as soldiers from France, Spain and Britain. During the Haitian revolution, France lost about 50,000 soldiers. This figure includes those killed in battle and those who died as a result of disease, particularly from yellow fever. On January 1, 1804, Dessalines declared independence, establishing the world's first Black republic and becoming the country's first Head of State. To eliminate traces of the old system, he named the new republic *Haiti* (formerly spelt Hayti), after the island's indigenous Arawak people. On September 22, 1804, the generals of the Haitian Revolutionary Army declared him Emperor and gave him the name *Jacques I of Haiti*.

The declaration of Haitian independence angered key European powers, including the USA. Because they were all slave-holding nations, they refused to legally recognise a nation founded by former enslaved people. They ensured that Haiti did not participate in the Atlantic trade. European countries, including the UK, Germany, France, Portugal, Spain, along with their counterparts in the USA, chose to isolate Haiti for fear that the newly independent country's success would inspire other rebellions and threaten their own dominance.

As a response, they imposed a boycott and embargo, damaging Haiti politically and economically. Western nations, such as the United States and the United Kingdom, continue to use this policy, now known as *sanctions*, as a major economic and political tool to enforce compliance with western policies and objectives.

Dessalines was undoubtedly the product of chattel slavery, which dehumanised him and all other enslaved Africans. This could explain why he had a great hatred for white people, particularly the French. His decision to remove the white band from the French flag, leaving just the blue and red as Haiti's colours, demonstrated how he linked independence to the eradication of whiteness in Haiti. Furthermore, the severity of Haiti's economic challenges, including an almost-collapsed agricultural sector due to the 1802-03 wars, combined with its isolation, had a significant impact on its export-driven economy. Many mulatto and free black landowners were outraged by his land *redistribution* policies. By late 1806, some of Dessalines' policies in response to Haiti's isolation were seen as authoritarian, resulting in his ambush and assassination by a group of rebels on October 17, 1806. The exact reasons for his death are unknown. However, it is widely suspected that Dessalines' rivals, including major mulattoe landowners and some of his own generals, were involved in the plot that led to his death. After Dessalines' assassinated, Haiti was divided into two halves, each with their own governments. The northern half was ruled by General Henry Christophe, president of the State of Haiti, while Alexandre Pétion was presided over the Republic of Haiti, which encompassed the southern and western regions.

In 1825, many years after Dessalines' death and several failed attempts to recolonise Haiti, which had reunified in 1821 under Jean-Pierre Boyer, the French returned with warships and demanded that Haiti pay a huge *indemnity* of 150 million-francs, which "is about $21 billion in present-day U.S. dollars" (Sperling, 2017, as cited in Fernandez, K. et al, 2021), to compensate former plantation/slave owners for the loss of their slaves and revenue from slavery. In exchange,

France agreed to recognise Haitian independence and halt French threats of invasion. Ironically, French bank Crédit Industriel et Commercial [C.I.C] and US bank National City Bank of New York (now Citibank) financed the debt at highly excessive interest rates, which was finally repaid in 1947. Haiti has yet to recover from its imposed debt and is still the poorest country in the Western Hemisphere. Instead of addressing the issues of racial oppression and colonialism, most European historians and many across the Americas saw Dessalines' war as an example of African barbarism, rather than a fight for freedom. Dessalines and his people's willingness to fight for life, liberty and the pursuit of happiness was severely punished, whereas atrocities committed by France and other European nations seemed to be ignored and overlooked. While some may question Dessalines' radical approach, it appears that he did whatever it took to free his people from slavery and French colonial rule.

Statute of Jean-Jacques Dessalines

Non-Haitian historians and authors may have disregarded Dessalines' achievements in favour of Toussaint L'Ouverture, but many Haitians and black nationalists consider Dessalines as the *father of independence*. Every year, the anniversary of his death (October 17) is observed as a national holiday, and "Haiti's national anthem, the *Dessalinienne*, is named after him" (Girard, 2012). Furthermore, in September 2021, the Haitian government declared September 20 each year as a national holiday to celebrate the birthday of Jean-Jacques Dessalines. The Haitian Revolution, led by Dessalines and others, was unprecedented in history. It established the second independent country in the Americas, after the USA, and it is still remembered as one of the most remarkable revolutions, with far-reaching consequences felt throughout the Americas, especially in Ecuador, Colombia and Venezuela.

These countries were part of the former state of Gran Colombia, and Dessalines' Haiti influenced and supported their revolution.

Marcos Xiorro (unknown-unknown)

The Taínos, an indigenous Arawak sub-group from the Caribbean and Florida (USA), inhabited Puerto Rico (then known as Borikén) during Christopher Columbus' second voyage to the New World in 1493. When he arrived, he claimed the island for the Spanish Crown, and in 1508, Juan Ponce de León founded the first Spanish settlement. Given Puerto Rico's strategic location as a military outpost to protect Spain's New World Empire, as well as its wealth, the Spanish proceeded to conquer the Taínos and this was completed after the 1511 Taino rebellion. Afterwards, the Taino people were forced to work as slaves in the gold mines and in the construction of military fortifications. Because of rising demand for goods and a decline in the indigenous population's ability to mine for gold and work the land, Spain decided to ship African captives to Puerto Rico. This occurred after African slavery was legalised in the Spanish Caribbean in 1501.

The first African captives landed in Puerto Rico around 1513. However, records show that when Puerto Rico was first colonised in the early 1500s, Spanish conquistadors were accompanied by free and formerly enslaved West African men who had previously lived in Spain, as well as those born in Iberian kingdoms. Juan Garrido was the first black man (born in West African) to set foot on the island of Puerto Rico, in 1509. He was apparently a member of conquistador Juan Ponce de León's entourage. African captives who later arrived came from a number of West and Central African ethnic groups. They were forced to travel through the unimaginable horrors of the Middle Passage to work in gold mines, replacing the indigenous Taino population, who were dying from overwork or European infectious diseases such as smallpox, measles and influenza. In such a labour-intensive environment, Africans' strength and resilience were highly valued, as evidenced by a letter from a San Juan attorney to Charles V in 1534 that stated, "We cannot live without Black people [slaves]" (Stark 2009).

In 1570, the Spanish settlers realised that the gold supply was running low and decided to start exploiting the fertile land by growing cash crops, such as sugar cane, coffee, ginger and tobacco. By the 1740s, sugar production in Puerto Rico had risen, necessitating the forced introduction and enslavement of additional Africans to work the land. Enslaved Africans, like those in all other slave/plantation societies, were abused and exploited for their labour. Some researchers believe that enslaved people in Puerto Rico adapted and accepted their situation, with only a few isolated incidents of uprisings without a leader or conspiracy. This could explain why it was assumed that enslaved Africans were *docile* and had no reason to rebel because they were well-cared for. It was clearly false, "as [Guillermo] Baralt [1982 book and reproduced in 2007] registers twenty-two episodes of collective slave resistance from 1795 to 1848, with the 1820s and 1840s as the principal periods of slave insubordination."

The first major slave uprising by enslaved Africans on the island of Puerto Rico took place in 1527, when some enslaved Africans fled to the forests and mountains to live as maroons alongside the remaining indigenous Taíno people. The subsequent uprisings and conspiracies were minor and mostly involved small rebel groups. However, in 1821, Marcos Xiorro rose to prominence as Puerto Rico's most famous conspirator and revolt planner, cementing his place in Puerto Rican folklore. Aside from the fact that he was brought from Africa, little is known about his childhood. Like all other African-born enslaved people, he was called *Bozal*, which means *wild* or *untamed*. His exploits showed that enslaved Africans were not passive or moldable labourers; like all human beings, they desired freedom. Xiorro's planned revolt on 29th July, 1821 was aimed at the sugar plantation owners and the Spanish Colonial authority in Puerto Rico. The proposed plot consisted of several enslaved people from various plantations, with Marcos Xiorro and a few others in charge of the operation. It also involved finding hidden weapons, setting fire to the town and slashing the throats of all white people. After that, they would join forces with other enslaved people from neighbouring towns. Apart from their inherent desire for freedom, they were also driven by the belief that the king and Parliament of Spain had freed all blacks, but that this information was being kept hidden by local powerful land owners. However, they were rumours and not true.

Unfortunately, Xiorro's rebellion plot was discovered by a loyal slave who notified his owner. This led to the despatch of about 500 Spanish soldiers by the Mayor of Bayamon, and they immediately arrested the conspirators. On August 15, 1812, the trials ended, with sixty-one rebel slaves sentenced and two ringleaders executed. Marcos was captured afterwards and tried separately. What happened to him is unknown, however he is thought to have been executed. Even though Marcos' plot was foiled, others continued to try. Historical records show that enslaved Africans made several more attempts to free themselves from slavery on numerous occasions, notably in 1812, 1821, 1826, 1841, 1843, and twice in 1848. As news of slave conspiracies and revolts grew in Puerto Rico, a repressive and punitive decree known as the *black code* was issued to prevent a full-fledged black revolution. Despite these racist laws and harsh penalties, enslaved people continued in their resistance. Another little-known fact is that until 1846, all Black people on the island, free and enslaved, were required to carry a notebook known as *Libreta* with them at all times. This was similar to the passbook system in South Africa during the apartheid (a system of segregation or discrimination against the black majority) era. Today's Afro or Black Puerto Ricans, many of whom are descended from the Yoruba, Igbo, Ashanti, Fon, Bambara, Wolof, Mandinka and the Kongo (aka Bakongo) people, have numerous reasons to be proud of their African ancestors. They did not only resist slavery, but also helped in shaping Puerto Rico's political, economic and cultural structures. Their contributions and heritage are still evident in Puerto Rico's art, music, dance forms, cuisine and religious beliefs.

Nat Turner (1800-1831)

Nat Turner was born into slavery on October 2, 1800, in Southampton County, Virginia, USA. He is best known for leading the deadliest slave rebellion in US history. Turner's enslaved mother was born in Africa and involuntarily brought to Norfolk, Virginia, around 1797. She had a tremendous influence in shaping his identity, which included glorifying the greatness of his African heritage and voicing strong opposition to slavery. Turner knew little about his father, but he is believed to have escaped from slavery when Turner was a young boy. Growing up in the backwaters of Southampton County, Virginia, Turner felt surrounded by a terrible system that dehumanised his people and condemned them to perpetual servitude.

Nat Turner was a clever young man who was curious, observant and eager to learn. As a result, he was taught to read and write, despite the fact that such activities were forbidden among the enslaved population. Turner was raised as a deeply religious person who spent a lot of time reading the Bible and preaching to his fellow enslaved people. He believed that he was "ordained for some great purpose in the hands of the Almighty" (Turner and Gray, 1831). Turner fled the plantation where he was born in 1821, at the aged 21, when an authoritarian overseer was appointed to further abuse the enslaved people. He returned thirty days later, surprising the entire slave community, which assumed he had successfully escaped, as his father had done in the past. His return seemed to be driven by a vision telling him that he had bigger plans and a greater destiny to accomplish. In another vision, many years after being sold to a new owner, Turner was instructed to rise and prepare to defeat his enemies with their own weapons. However, the appearance of a solar eclipse in February

REBEL LEADERS

1831 warned him that the time to rise was fast approaching. He then revealed his rebellion plans to the four men he trusted the most. Turner, like many other revolutionary figures, wanted nothing more than to eliminate slavery, thereby putting an end to racism, injustice and white supremacy.

During the rebellion's planning stage, Turner strategically and methodically recruited some of his most loyal followers into his inner circle. He was also able to persuade a few others from nearby farms and plantations to join his cause. On August 21, 1831, Nat Turner and about 70 armed enslaved men and free blacks went on a killing spree from plantation to plantation. They seized guns and horses, rescuing and recruiting others along the way. Their purpose was to kill every white person they came across and eventually take over Southampton's county seat, Jerusalem (present-day Courtland, Virginia). According to reports, between 55 and 60 white people were killed during Turner's two-day revolt. The insurgency was put down within 48 hours by federal troops and militias, and the majority of the rebels were captured, with the exception of Turner. In an effort to avenge the white killings, angry mobs lynched a large number of innocent black people. Historians estimate that almost 200 enslaved people were killed. Moreover, the 55 people suspected of taking part in the revolt were executed, and the state compensated slave owners for their property losses. It took the authorities two months to capture Turner.

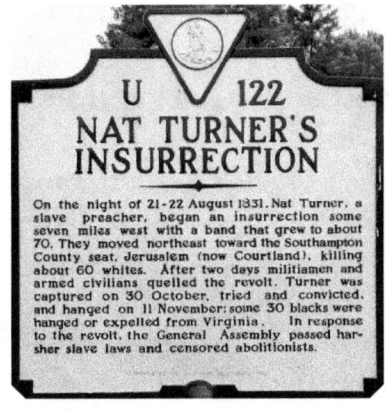

Historical Highway Marker Listing of Nat Turner's Rebellion

Turner's *confessions* were recorded inside his cell in the Southampton County jailhouse by Thomas Gray on November, 1, the day after his capture; he was convicted on November 5, and hanged from a tree in the town of Jerusalem on November 11, 1831. Turner's declaration to Thomas Gray, contained in *The Confessions of Nat Turner*, stated that he believed he had received divine visions to avenge slavery and free his people from bondage. He claimed that his mother and grandmother instilled in him the desire to become a prophet from an early age. This was something he remembered when explaining why he had planned the rebellion. Following the revolt, strict laws were passed to control the lives of black people (both free and enslaved), restricting their ability to read, write and move around. What happened to Turner's body is unclear; however, in an article in the *Journal of Negro History*, John W. Cromwell wrote, "Turner was skinned to supply such souvenirs as purses, his flesh made into grease, and his bones divided as trophies to be handed down as heirlooms" (Cromwell, 1920). Nat Turner's insurrection may not have achieved its ultimate goal, but it dispelled the *white myth* that enslaved Africans were either content or happy with their situation, or incapable of waging an armed revolution. Nat Turner stood up against his and his people's oppression. His revolt had a tremendous impact on the slave system in Virginia and other Southern states. Nat Turner is mostly remembered as a revolutionary who believed in liberty.

Samuel Sharpe (c.1801-1832)

Samuel [Sam] Sharpe was an enslaved black Jamaican preacher and abolitionist who led the largest slave revolt ever witnessed in the British Caribbean. This massive uprising erupted in the island's western parishes in 1831 and became known as the Baptist War (aka the Christmas Rebellion or the Sam Sharpe Rebellion). It helped to change the course of slavery in Britain's Caribbean territories. Sharpe was born into slavery in the parish of St James, Jamaica, and grew up on a plantation owned by Samuel and Jane Sharpe. According to the plantation documents from 1817, he lived as a trusted *house slave* alongside his mother and two siblings. Sam Sharpe was allowed to learn to read, and other enslaved people looked up to him. He was supposedly well-treated, given certain *privileges*, and eventually became his owner's right-hand man. Sharpe rose to prominence as a preacher and leader in the Baptist Church, which at the time accepted enslaved Africans as members and recognised their preaching ability. Furthermore, he was known as *Daddy* because of his knowledge and leadership qualities, and he served as deacon at the local church in Montego Bay, St. James.

Sam Sharpe's exceptional oratory skills allowed him to preach religious doctrines to the enslaved people while also informing them about events in Jamaica and the issue of freedom from slavery. He used his position as a preacher to attend religious gatherings in and around Montego Bay to explain his non-violent resistance plan, which called for enslaved people to refuse to work after the three-day Christmas holidays (December 25-27) in 1831. This would be the case until plantation owners agreed to their demands for improved living conditions, better treatment and the consideration of freedom. At this same time, the call for abolition was fast growing in Britain, and the non-conformist Christian churches, particularly the Baptists, were committed in their fight against slavery. This enraged slave owners, who became increasingly resistant and critical of the British Government's efforts to improve living conditions for the enslaved population. They then explored the prospect of breaking away from Britain. However, it never came to fruition. Sharpe's non-violent work stoppage or *sit down strike* quickly erupted into a large-scale revolt on December 27, 1831, when the *Great House* on the Kensington estate in St. James was set on fire. This was unknown to Sam Sharpe, and it was followed by a series of fires started by dissident enslaved rebels.

The horrific devastation on Kensington estate ignited the rebellion, which swept through the western parishes from St. James to Manchester, destroying many sugar cane fields and plantations. This scared the white people, who feared for their lives. The revolt was eventually crushed by local militiamen and British troops stationed in Jamaica. Economic hardship, poor working conditions, a desire for freedom, and the mistaken belief that the British Parliament had granted enslaved people freedom, but local plantation owners refused to comply, all contributed to the rebellion. The insurrection reportedly cost more than £1 million in property damage and involved 60,000 of Jamaica's 300,000 enslaved people. According to Fiddes and Kreitzer (2024), "over eight days about 14 white overseers or planters and 186 slaves were killed." They further claimed that during the subsequent trials, over 500 enslaved people were executed. Hamilton (2024) argues that "the official toll seriously underestimates the number of people who lost their lives."

Sam Sharpe was a religious man who believed that white men were not superior to black men and opposed the idea that white people had the right to enslave black people. He quoted specific Bible verses to support his assertion. On May 23, 1832, he and other ringleaders were tried, convicted and hanged. Sharpe's rebellion may not have achieved the desired results, but it clearly sent a message to British officials that slavery was no longer viable in the British Caribbean. Many people seem to believe that the Christmas Rebellion of 1831 accelerated the passing of the Slavery Abolition Act 1833 by the British Parliament, resulting in the abolition of slavery throughout the British Empire a year later. It demonstrated that Jamaica's enslaved population would no longer accept slavery. Sharpe's extraordinary bravery and unwavering fighting spirit while facing death on the gallows lasted until the end. Just before being execution, he said, "I would rather die upon yonder gallows than live in slavery."

Following Sam Sharpe's execution, his owners received £16 pounds and 10 shillings in compensation for their loss of property. He was initially buried as a criminal in the sands of the Montego Bay Harbour, but his body was later exhumed and reburied beneath the pulpit of Burchell Memorial Baptist Church in Montego Bay. Surprisingly, Sam Sharpe received a tribute from a plantation owner who opposed him and the rebellion. He described Sharpe as "active, intelligent and subtle" (Fiddes and Kreitzer, 2024). Sam Sharpe was posthumously named a National Hero of Jamaica in 1975 and awarded the Order of the National Hero in 1982. His image can be found on the old Jamaican $50 banknote, however, he is currently featured on the new $500 bill alongside Nanny of the Maroons. In 1976, Charles Square in Montego Bay was renamed Sam Sharpe Square in honour of his life and the courage he displayed in his efforts to abolish slavery in Jamaica. A few years later, several bronze monuments depicting Sharpe holding his Bible and ministering to his people were erected.

Carlota Lukumi (unknown-1843)

Carlota Lukumi (aka *La Negra Carlota*) was an enslaved woman who led a revolt against Spanish forces in Cuba. Little is known about her early life, as is true for most enslaved people. According to sources, Carlota was born in West Africa and is descended from the Yoruba ethnic group of present-day Nigeria and the Benin Republic. Interestingly, when European slave traders brought Yorubas to the Americas (particularly in Cuba) in the 17th century, they renamed them *Lukumi* (often spelt *Lucumi*) after the expression *olukumi*, which means *my friend*, which they often used to greet or welcome one another. Carlota is said to have been kidnapped as a child, sold into slavery in Matanzas (Cuba), and forced to endure a terrible and brutal life. As noted by Ramos (2013), the Yorubas are one of the three major African ethnic groups that have had a significant impact on the island's *Cubanidad* (national identity). The other two groups were the *Congos*, a Bantu speaking ethnic group from Central West Africa and the *Carabalis* from the Bight of Biafra, a region that includes southeastern Nigeria and the Cameroons in West Africa. During the early 1900s, these enslaved groups faced attacks on their cultural identity and way of life. However, the Lukumies were mostly responsible for fighting back. They used a variety of violent tactics to oppose slavery. Some considered them passive or submissive, while others thought they were honourable and hardworking. What was certain at the time was that the arrival of the Lukumies coincided with an increase in slave revolts on the island of Cuba.

Following the victory of the Haitian Revolution led by enslaved Africans in 1804, Cuba rose to become the world's largest sugar producer by 1830. This resulted in a record number of African captives being imported, and they were pushed to their limits. These enslaved individuals endured harsh working conditions and cruel treatment. The severity of the slave system motivated Carlota to lead an uprising among her fellow oppressed people. Her role in organising a plot that would normally be dominated by men could be attributed to the fact that "at least half of slaves imported [to Cuba] after 1830 were women." (Peter, 2010). Many of these women would have had to take on additional responsibilities, not just domestic tasks, but also at sugar mills and plantations. Carlota developed the plan with Fermina, another enslaved woman and fellow Lukumi who was eventually arrested for spreading information about the conspiracy. When her actions were discovered, Fermina was severely beaten, shackled and imprisoned. This caused Carlota to reconsider her strategy, and she began sending out secret and coded messages via *talking drums* (West African traditional instruments), encouraging other enslaved people on surrounding farms and plantations to join the rebellion.

On November 5, 1843, Carlota and other *Triumvirato Rebellion* leaders led a group of warrior enslaved Africans armed with machetes in a revolt against the Triunvirato sugar plantation owners and others in the area. Her first objective was to free Fermina and a dozen others from captivity. The group then set fire to several houses, including those used to imprison and torture enslaved people. As the uprising spread, more Africans joined the cause. According to slave testimony, their goal was "to go to the farms, gather together the greatest possible number of slaves, make war on the whites, become free, and not do any work" (Fleishman, 2013). The Triumvirato Rebellion was one of several African-led slave revolts that began in 1825 and continued until the mid-1840s. After two days of fighting, which claimed the lives of some whites and destroyed at least five sugar plantations, the Spanish governor dispatched troops, who eventually defeated the rebels. This led to the arrest of Carlota and some of her other collaborators. On the night of her capture, colonial repressive forces tied Carlota to horses and sent them running in opposite directions. The next morning, her followers discovered her destroyed and unrecognisable body, and the news of her death sparked further uprisings in the hope of completing the task of liberating enslaved Africans.

For the majority of 1844, slave owners, fearful of a repeat of the Haitian Revolution, imposed a savage wave of tyrannical laws that prosecuted and brutalised anyone of African descent, enslaved or free. The government tortured, executed and expelled dissidents, including Fermina, who was shot dead in March 1844. The military shot hundreds of black men in the back and mutilated their heads. The year 1844 became known as the *Year of the Lash*. This situation was similar to the 1521 Santo Domingo Slave Revolt, which began on the sugar-making plantation owned by Diego Columbus (aka Diego Colón and Diego Colombo), Christopher Columbus' son. After the Spaniards put down the revolt, many of the rebels were killed, while others committed suicide to avoid capture. To maintain the slave system, the Spanish authorities enacted punitive laws in 1522, just ten days after crushing the revolt. These harsh laws became the first versions of *Black Codes* in the Americas, and they were intended to limit the rights of all black people, enslaved or not. Their goal was to control and prevent similar events from taking place again.

Statue of Carlota Lukumi

Carlota's death and the atrocities committed against African descendants did not completely dampen their spirits, as there were several conspiratorial attempts to abolish slavery. Incidentally, people of

African descent, aka Afro Cubans, fought in the *Ten Years' War* (1868-78) to secure Cuba's independence from Spain. Though the 1843 slave revolt failed, it instilled a permanent fear among whites on the island of Cuba and set a historical precedent. Carlota's revolt, like many others in the 19th century, is thought to have influenced Fidel Castro's (Cuba's leader from 1959-2008) ideology, which held that the oppressed would rise up to defeat their oppressor. The revolutionary government of Cuba named a military operation in Angola *Black Carlota* in support of the People's Movement for the Liberation of Angola (MPLA), after this remarkable Yoruba female warrior. The operation resulted in the defeat of the South African army, which facilitated negotiations to end Apartheid in South Africa. Carlota's statue stands proud over the ruins of the Triumvirato sugar mill. Her life exemplifies African women's courage and leadership qualities, especially those who led rebellions during a time when rebel leaders were mostly men.

> *"[To anyone or group of persons enslaved,] let your motto be resistance! Resistance! RESISTANCE! No oppressed people have ever secured their liberty without resistance."*
> —HENRY HIGHLAND GARNET

STATUES OF REBEL LEADERS

From L-R Top: Gaspar Yanga, Jean-Jacques Dessalines
From L-R Bottom: Ganga Zumbi, Abeng (Cow Horn) - an Akan cultural instrument used as a symbol of freedom by the Maroons in the Caribbean, Nanny of the Maroons

CHAPTER FOUR

CONCLUSION

The notorious trans-Atlantic slave trade, described as *the most massive demographic event in modern history*, established a system of slavery that was both commercially driven and racially motivated. Under the chattel slavery system, enslaved Africans were treated as commodities to be purchased, sold and exploited rather than as human beings. Its scale, scope and cruelty were unprecedented, making it one of the worst crimes against humanity. Nonetheless, Africans opposed slavery at forts, along the coast, on board ships and on plantations. The resistance took many forms, from individual acts of defiance to organised rebellions. They engaged in acts of sabotage and insubordination, plotted and revolted, and formed large and small maroon communities that disrupted the institution of slavery. The fight against chattel slavery involved both violent and non-violent actions. The former received extensive coverage, while the latter received little attention, despite the fact that it was widespread and occurred on a daily basis. During slavery, it was estimated that children accounted for one-quarter of people involuntarily taken from Africa. These children, like their adult counterparts, went through the same traumatic event. Slave owners expected that the children would easily adapt to the slave system and abandon their cultural heritage, but this was clearly not the case. It must have come as a shock to them when the likes of Carlota Lukumi, Prince Klaas and Francois Mackandal, as adults, took on the responsibility of attempting to free themselves and their people from slavery.

CONCLUSION

Enslaved Africans understood the true meaning of freedom, as many came from a *warrior tradition*. This explains why, upon arrival in the Americas, they worked tirelessly to regain their humanity, as opposed to the myth perpetuated by many European writers who falsely claimed that Africans were *genetically* docile, subservient and supplicant (someone who begs or prays for something). Despite the use of violence to put down rebellions and conspiracies, Africans resisted. For example, Ganga Zumbi, Benkos Biohó, Gaspar Yanga, and many others who appear to have been overlooked or forgotten by history risked their lives to escape the horrors of plantation life and establish communities in often hostile environments. They are unquestionable advocates for liberation and self-determination in the Americas. While most Maroon societies have disappeared or been integrated into larger communities, those in Suriname, French Guiana and Jamaica still exist today. African descendants around the world can learn a lot about maroon communities by looking into historical records, including oral histories. The maroons' experiences show that many communities remained resolute and resilient, believing that their collective unity was their strength.

The power of African spirituality remained evident throughout African enslavement in the Americas. Because their enslavers failed to provide for their basic needs, enslaved Africans were forced to rely on their own traditions and spiritual practices to tackle spiritual matters and treat various illnesses. In addition, African spiritual systems, such as Santeria and Vodou, which Europeans referred to as *devilish religions*, played an essential role in the fight against slavery. They were closely connection with slave resistance and rebellions. Rebel leaders, such as Nanny of the Maroons, Francois Mackandal and Prince Klaas protected and motivated their followers by passing down spiritual practices from their ancestors. As a result, the Haitian revolution, whose version of obeah is known as Vodou, demonstrates the powerful nature of African spiritual practices, as the majority of the enslaved African population chose to believe in the God of their ancestors over that of their oppressors. The outcome was a historic victory over France and other major European powers, as well as the founding of Haiti, the Western Hemisphere's first independent black African nation.

On reflection, the slave revolts organised by enslaved Africans, both successful and unsuccessful, were extremely significant because they put pressure on those who perpetuated slavery against them and demonstrated that Africans would go to any length to obtain freedom. Many of these revolts or conspiracies to revolt involved betrayal by certain enslaved individuals in order to appease their white enslavers and the larger white society. This painful habit of *selling out* has been a recurring theme since slavery and remains a stain on modern black/African society. Despite efforts by colonial historians to downplay the significance of the numerous uprisings and revolts that began on the coast of West Africa, spread to slave ships and swept across the Americas, they all contributed to abolish the colonial system of chattel slavery. With the intensity and frequency with which enslaved people organised and led revolts, some white politicians in the 1800s realised that slavery could no longer be ignored and had to be abolished. Africans and African descendants who risked their lives by actively participating in insurgencies and changing the narrative through publications and speeches deserve to be recognised, commended and honoured. As a result of their selfless agitation, black people were able to restore their human dignity, which had been taken away during the period of the trans-Atlantic slave trade.

Enslaved Africans opposed captivity in every way possible in order to preserve their African identity. The victory of the Haitian revolution, which echoed throughout the Americas and Europe, served as a constant reminder of the possibility that enslaved people can rise up and free themselves. It is worth mentioning that many great Africans or people of African ancestry featured in this book were driven by a desire for freedom, not a fear of death. Therefore, it is historically correct to conclude that emancipation was ultimately achieved primarily through the efforts and perseverance of these black-African

CONCLUSION

abolitionists and their descendants, many of whom risked and sacrificed their lives in various forms of resistance, significantly contributing to the anti-slavery movement that emerged in the late 18th Century. Their persistent commitment to freedom influenced and fuelled white abolitionist efforts and arguments against slavery, compelling European slave-trading nations to pass legislation abolishing the horrific, cruel and barbaric system of chattel slavery. An important takeaway from Thompson's 2006 study was that descendants of enslaved Africans (numbering about 200 million people) in the Americas must "guard against threats to the freedoms that our ancestors won by sweat and blood," and that if they fail to learn from the past, history will most likely repeat itself.

> "Africans in the United States [and across the diaspora] must remember that the slave ships brought no West Indians, no Caribbeans, no Jamaicans or Trinidadians or Barbadians to this hemisphere. The slave ships brought only African people and most of us took the semblance of nationality from the places where slave ships dropped us off."
>
> —JOHN HENRIK CLARKE

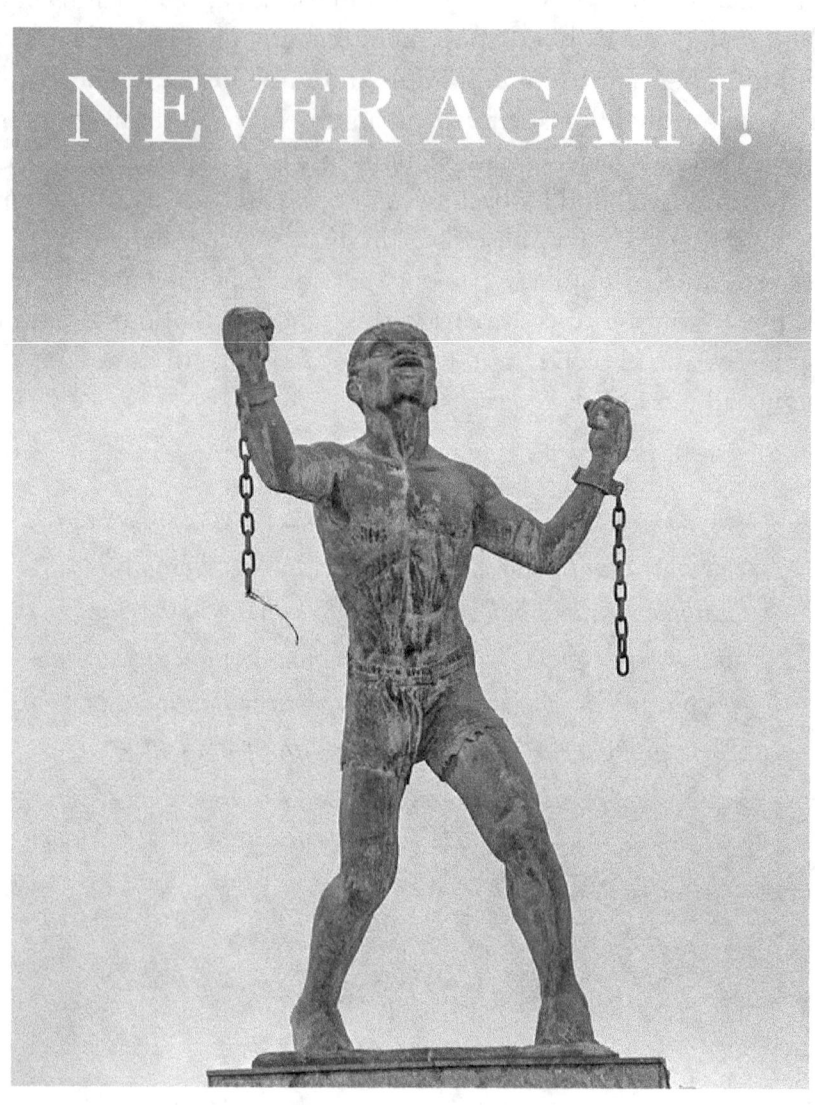

Statue Commemorating The Life And Struggle of Bussa. In 1861, He Led The Last And Largest Slave Rebellion In Barbados

RECORDS OF SOME SLAVE REVOLTS IN THE AMERICAS

NO	YEAR	NAME OF REVOLT	LOCATION
1	1521	Santo Domingo Slave Revolt	Santo Domingo, Hispaniola
2	1526	San Miguel de Guadalpe	Spanish Florida, USA
3	1548–58, 1579–82	Bayano Wars	Panama, New Spain
4	c.1570	Gaspar Yanga's Revolt	Veracruz, New Spain [colonial Mexico]
5	1656	Guadeloupe Slave Revolt	Guadeloupe, French Caribbean
6	1675	Barbados Slave Rebellion	British Barbados
7	1678	Martinique Slave Revolt	French Caribbean
8	1712	New York Slave Revolt	British Province of New York
9	1728-1739	First Maroon War	British Jamaica
10	1733	St. John (Danish: St. Jan) Slave Revolt	Danish Saint John
11	1739	Stono Rebellion	British Province of South Carolina, USA
12	1741	New York City Conspiracy	British Province of New York
13	1757	Tempati Rebellion	Suriname
14	1760	Tacky's Rebellion	British Jamaica
15	1763	Berbice Slave Revolt	Guyana

NO	YEAR	NAME OF REVOLT	LOCATION
16	1765-1793	Boni Maroon Wars	Suriname
17	1769-1773	First [black] Carib War	St. Vincent
18	1770	Sandy's Rebellion	Tobago
19	1787	Abaco Slave Revolt	British Bahamas
20	1789	[West] Demerara Rebellion	Dutch Demerara [Guyana]
21	1791	Mina Conspiracy	Louisiana New Spain
22	1791–1804	Haitian Revolution	French Saint-Domingue
23	1795	Pointe Coupée Conspiracy	Louisiana New Spain
24	1795	Curaçao Slave Revolt	Dutch Curaçao
25	1795	Fédon's Rebellion	Grenada
26	1795	Coro Rebellion	Venezuela
27	1795-1796	Second Maroon War	British Jamaica
28	1795-1797	Second [black] Carib War	St. Vincent
29	1800	Gabriel's Conspiracy	Virginia, USA
30	1803	Igbo [landing] Slave Revolt	St. Simons Island, Georgia, USA
31	1805	Chatham Manor	Virginia, USA
32	1811	German Coast Uprising	Territory of Orleans, USA
33	1812	The Aponte conspiracy	Cuba
34	1815	George Boxley	Virginia, USA
35	1816	Bussa's Rebellion	British Barbados
36	1821	Marcos Xiorro Conspiracy	Spanish Puerto Rico
37	1822	Denmark Vesey	South Carolina, USA

RECORDS OF SOME SLAVE REVOLTS IN THE AMERICAS

NO	YEAR	NAME OF REVOLT	LOCATION
38	1823	The [East coast] Demerara Rebellion	British Demerara (Guyana)
39	1825	Matanzas Rebellion	Cuba
40	1831	Nat Turner's Rebellion	Virginia, USA
41	1831-1832	Baptist War	British Jamaica
42	1833	Carrancas Revolt	Minas Gerais, Brazil
43	1835	Malê Revolt	Brazil
44	1835-1838	Black Seminole Slave Rebellion	Central Florida, USA
45	1839	Amistad, Ship Mutiny	Off the Cuban coast
46	1848	Emancipation Revolt	Danish West Indies

BIBLIOGRAPHY

1. Ali, O.M. (2018). African and Afro-Indian Rebel Leaders in Latin America: Con Tanta Arrogancia [with such arrogance]. Revista: *Harvard Review of Latin America*, 17 (2). https://revista.drclas.harvard.edu/african-and-afro-indian-rebel-leaders-in-latin-america/
2. Appiah, A., ed. (1990). *Early African-American Classics*. London: Bantam Books
3. Ball, L. (2013). *Memory, Myth and Forgetting: the British Transatlantic Slave Trade*. [Ph.D. thesis, University of Portsmouth].
4. Baralt G, A. (2007). *Slave revolts in Puerto Rico: conspiracies and uprisings, 1795–1873*. Princeton: Markus Wiener Publishers.
5. Bellardie, T. and Heemskerk, M. (2019b). Maroons in French Guiana: History, culture, demographics, and socioeconomic development along the Maroni and Lawa Rivers. Available from: https://s24.q4cdn.com/382246808/files/doc_downloads/2021/06/French-Guiana-Maroons-June-7-2021.pdf (Accessed 3 April 2024).
6. Brooks, J. (2010). From Freedom to Bondage: The Jamaican Maroons, 1655-1770. *Explorations*, 5(29), 11.
7. Camargo, B., & Lawo-Sukam, A. (2015). San Basilio de Palenque (Re)visited: African Heritage, Tourism, and Development in Colombia. *Afro-Hispanic Review*, 34(1), 25-45.
8. Carey, B. (2003). William Wilberforce's Sentimental Rhetoric: Parliamentary Reportage and the Abolition Speech of 1789. In: Korshin, P.J. and Lynch, J. (eds.) *The Age of Johnson: A Scholarly Annual*, 14, New York: AMS Press, pp. 281-305.

9. Carey, B. 2003. The extraordinary Negro: Ignatius Sancho, Joseph Jekyll, and the Problem of Biography, *British Journal for Eighteenth-Century Studies*, 26(1), 1-13.

10. Clemente, R (2001, June 10,). *Who Is Black?* [Online]. Rosa Clemente, New York. Available from: https://rosaclemente.net/who-is-black/ (Accessed 21 April 2025).

11. Connell, R. (2017). The Political Ecology of Maroon Autonomy: Land, Resource Extraction and Political Change in 21st Century Jamaica and Suriname. [Ph.D. thesis, Berkeley University].

12. Cromwell J.W. (1920). The Aftermath of Nat Turner's Insurrection. *Journal of Negro History*, 5(2), 208-234.

13. Cugoano, Q.O. (1999). In: Carretta, V. (ed.) *Thoughts and Sentiments on the Evil of Slavery and Other Writings*. New York: Penguin Books.

14. Dash, M. (2013, January 2). *Antigua's Disputed Slave Conspiracy of 1736: Does the evidence against these 44 slaves really stack up?* [Online]. Washington, D.C., Smithsonian Magazine. Available from: https://www.smithsonianmag.com/history/antiguas-disputed-slave-conspiracy-of-1736-117569/ (Accessed 22 April 2025).

15. Daut, M.L. (2020). *The Wrongful Death of Toussaint Louverture: Toussaint Louverture's lonely death in a French prison cell was not an unfortunate tragedy but a cruel story of betrayal*. [Online]. London, History Today. Available from: https://www.historytoday.com/archive/feature/wrongful-death-toussaint-louverture (Accessed 15 March 2024).

16. Davidson, D.M. (1966). Negro Slave Control and Resistance in Colonial Mexico, 1519-1650. *Hispanic American Historical Review*, 46(3), 235-253.

17. Dawson, S. (2024). *Harriet Tubman-Davis*. [Online]. Washington, D.C., NWHM. Available from: https://www.womenshistory.org/education-resources/biographies/harriet-tubman (Accessed 10 Feb. 2025).

18. De Carvalho, A. V. (2007). Archaeological Perspectives of Palmares: A Maroon Settlement in 17th Century Brazil. The African Diaspora Archeaeology Newsletter, 10(1), 1-17.

19. Demony, C. (2023). *African, Caribbean nations join forces to call for reparations for slavery*. [Online]. London, Reuters. https://www.reuters.com/world/african-caribbean-nations-join-forces-call-reparations-slavery-2023-07-27/ (Accessed 01 Feb. 2025).

BIBLIOGRAPHY

20. Eddins, C. N. (2022). Consciousness and Interaction: Cultural Expressions, Networks and Ties, Geographies and Space. In: *Rituals, Runaways, and the Haitian Revolution: Collective Action in the African Diaspora*. Cambridge: Cambridge University Press, pp.109-240.
21. Egerton, D.R. (1990). Gabriel's Conspiracy and the Election of 1800. *The Journal of Southern History*, 56(2), 191-214.
22. Equal Justice Initiative (2023). *The Atlantic Slave Trade*. [Online]. Montgomery: EJI. Available from: https://eji.org/wp-content/uploads/2005/11/transatlantic-report-PDF-web.pdf (Accessed 20 January 2025).
23. Everett, S. (1978). *History of Slavery*. Reprint, Hong Kong: Bison Books Ltd, 1993.
24. Fernandez, K. et al. (2021). *France's Overdue Debt to Haiti*. [Online]. Philadelphia, SSRN. Available from: file:///C:/Users/pfamily/Downloads/ssrn-3798841.pdf (Accessed 24 November 2024).
25. Fick, C. E. (1990). *The Making of Haiti: The Saint-Domingue Revolution from Below*. Knoxville: The University of Tennessee Press.
26. Fiddes, P.S. & Kreitzer, L.J. (2024). Sam Sharpe: The Scriptures that Motivated Him and their Implications for Today, *Baptist Quarterly*, 55(3), 118-133.
27. Fleishman, E.S. (2013). *Sugar, Slavery, and Violence: the Moral Economy of Slaves on Nineteenth-Century Cuban Ingenios*. [Master's dissertation, University of Georgia].
28. Frederick, D. (1845). *Narrative of the Life of Frederick Douglass, an American Slave*. Boston: Anti-Slavery Office.
29. Gerbner, K.R. (2013). *Christian Slavery: protestant Missions and Slave Conversion in the Atlantic World, 1660-1760*. [Ph.D. thesis, Harvard University]. https://core.ac.uk/download/28943886.pdf
30. Girard, P. R. (2012) Jean-Jacques Dessalines and the Atlantic System: A Reappraisal. *The William and Mary Quarterly*, 69(3), 549-582.
31. Guillén, A. L. Z. (2018). *Geographies of Marronage: Dispossession and Resistance in the Last Palenque*. [Ph.D. thesis, Harvard University].
32. Hamilton, D. (2024). To prevent any succour to the insurgents': Enslaved insurgency and the Royal Navy in the Caribbean, 1795-1832. *International Journal of Maritime History*, 36(1), 51-72.

33. Jaramillo, D.R. (2008). Palenques and Benkos: Myth and reality to think about education. *Education and Humanism Magazine*, 15, 177-187.
34. Jenson, D. (2010). Dessalines's American proclamations of the Haitian independence. *The Journal of Haitian Studies*, 15, 72-102.
35. Karasch, M. (2013). Zumbi of Palmares: Challenging the Portuguese Colonial order. In: Andrien, K.J. (ed.). *The human tradition in colonial Latin America*. Wilmington, DE: Scholarly Resources, pp.104-120.
36. Kavon, K. (2018). Third Root of Mexico: Exploring Afro-Mexican History & Culture. [Online]. Belfast: Global Education Centre. Available from: https://www.globaleducationcenter.org/uploads/5/4/4/6/54461425/the_third_root_curriculum_guide.pdf (Accessed on 16 December 2024).
37. Killingray, D. (2007). Britain, the Slave Trade and Slavery: An African Hermeneutic, 1787, *Anvil*, 24(2), 121-136.
38. Koch, A, et al. (2019). Earth system impacts of the European arrival and Great Dying in the Americas after 1492. *Quaternary Science Reviews*, 207, 13-36.
39. Kolchin, P. (1993). *American slavery, 1619-1877*. New York: Hill and Wang
40. Konadu, K. (2010). *The Akan Diaspora in the Americas, Oxford*: Oxford University Press.
41. Krass, P. (1988). *Sojourner Truth, anti-slavery activist*. New York: Chelsea House Publishers.
42. Landers, J. (no date) "Maroon ethnicity and identity in Ecuador, Colombia, and Hispaniola." Available from: https://www.academia.edu/5854993/Maroon_Ethnicity_and_Identity_in_Ecuador_Colombia_and_Hispaniola (Accessed 25 October 2024).
43. Larson, K.C. (2003). *Asanti Daughter of Zion: The life and memory of Harriet Tubman*. [Ph.D. thesis, University of New Hampshire].
44. Lovejoy P. E. (2006). Autobiography and memory: Gustavus Vassa, alias Olaudah Equiano, the African. *Slavery & Abolition: A Journal of Slave and Post-Slave Studies*, 27 (3), 317-347.
45. Marcum, A., & Skarbek, D. (2014). Why Didn't Slaves Revolt More Often During the Middle Passage? *Rationality and Society*, 26(2), 236-262.
46. Matthews, D. (2014). *Six times victims have received reparations - including four in the US*. [Online]. Washington D.C., Vox. Available from: https://www.vox.com/2014/5/23/5741352/

six-times-victims-have-received-reparations-including-four-in-the-us (Accessed 24/02/2025).

47. Misiedjan, M. (2010). *The Ndyuka Treaty of 1760: A Conversation with Granman Gazon* [online]. Cambridge MA, Cultural Survival. Available from: https://www.culturalsurvival.org/publications/cultural-survival-quarterly/ndyuka-treaty-1760-conversation-granman-gazon (Accessed 20 November 2023).

48. Peters, C.A. (2010). *Identifying (with) 'Carlota': Myths, Metaphors and Landscapes of Cuban Africania, 1974-1980.* [Ph.D. thesis, University of Nottingham].

49. Polo, D. (2023). *PM slams morons against reparations for slavery.* [Online]. Port of Spain, T&T Guardian. Available from: https://www.guardian.co.tt/news/pm-slams-morons-against-reparations-for-slavery-6.2.1766378.f1b7f46b9b (Accessed 15/11/2024).

50. Prince, M. (2006) *The History of Mary Prince, A West Indian Slave.* [Online]. Salt Lake City, Project Gutenberg. Available from: https://gutenberg.org/files/17851/17851-h/17851-h.htm (Accessed 13/12/2024).

51. Ramos, M. (2013). *Lucumí (Yoruba) Culture in Cuba: A Reevaluation (1830S -1940s).* [Ph.D. thesis, Florida International University].

52. Rangel, J.A. (2022). *Infographic: Afrodescendants in Mexico.* [Online]. Washington, D.C., Wilson Center. Available from: https://www.wilsoncenter.org/article/infographic-afrodescendants-mexico (Accessed 6/12/2024).

53. Roberts, A. (2024). *Portugal's debate over colonial and slavery reparations resurfaces.* BBC [online]. London, BBC. Available from: https://www.bbc.co.uk/news/world-europe-68916320 (Accessed 28 Jan. 2025).

54. Ruuth, Marianne. (1991). *Frederick Douglass: Patriot and Activist.* Los Angeles: Melrose Square Publishing Company.

55. Shabaka, L.H. (2013) *Transformation of "old" slavery into Atlantic slavery: Cape Verde Islands, C. 1500–1879.* [Ph.D. thesis, Michigan State University].

56. Sherman-Peter, M. (2022). The legacy of slavery in the Caribbean and the journey towards justice. *United Nations Chronicle.* [Online]. New York, United Nations. Available from: https://www.un.org/en/un-chronicle/legacy-slavery-caribbean-and-journey-towards-justice (Accessed 06/02/2025).

57. Sherwood, M. (1992). *Black peoples in the Americas*. London: The Savannah Press.
58. Somerville, Laura B. (1994). Gentle student bend thine ear to my speech. An Essay about Sojourner Truth, abolitionist and feminist. *The Journal of Sociology & Social Welfare*, 21(1).
59. Stark, D.M (2006). A new look at the African slave trade in Puerto Rico through the use of parish registers: 1660-1815. *Slavery and Abolition*, 30 (4), 491-520.
60. Thompson, A.O. (2006). *Flight to Freedom: African Runaways and Maroons in the Americas*. Kingston: University of the West Indies Press.
61. Tita, C. (2023). Ignatius Sancho's letters of the late Ignatius Sancho, an African (1782): race and nation as a rhetoric of resistance (Article). *Studies in Religion and the Enlightenment*, 3(1), 53-67.
62. Turner, N., & Gray, T.R. (1831). *The Confessions of Nat Turner*. Baltimore: T.R. Gray.
63. van Andel, T., Maat, H., & Pinas, N. (2024). Maroon women in Suriname and French Guiana: rice, slavery, memory. *Slavery and Abolition*, 45(2), 187-211.
64. White, L. (2001). *Stedman's Narrative: Its Origins & Transformations*. [Ph.D. thesis, Universidade Aberta].
65. Winkelman, W. (1976). *Barbadian Cross-currents: Church-State Confrontation with Quaker and Negro, 1660-1689*. [Ph.D. thesis, Loyola University Chicago].
66. Wood, B. (2002). *Slavery in Colonial Georgia*. [Online]. Cambridge, New Georgia Encyclopedia. Available from: https://www.georgiaencyclopedia.org/articles/history-archaeology/slavery-in-colonial-georgia/ (Accessed on 14 March 2024).

FURTHER READING:

Books to Educate, Inspire and Empower by Michael Nathan-Pepple

AmaZing Africa seeks to change the narrative by telling the African story. It aims to inform, educate and enlighten readers about Africa through twenty-six African related characters such as Alkebulan, Cowrie Shells, Drum, Queen, Pyramid and Zimbabwe. The book is essentially an A-Z resource guide about Africa.

Review: *It is a fascinating book with a wealth of information that I was previously unaware of. It is nice to know the real facts. Thank you.*

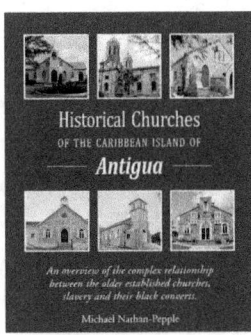

Historical Churches of the Caribbean Island of Antigua examines the complex relationship between the Older Established Churches, slavery and the conversion of enslaved Africans to Christianity. It also includes beautiful photographs and information about each historical church featured in the book. The experience in Antigua and Barbuda mirrors what occurred throughout the Caribbean region and the Americas as a whole.

Reviews: *"The book explores the positive educational and social impact of these institutions, and doesn't sanitise the murkier parts of the church history as relates to Black people in Antigua and Barbuda."*

"This is truly a long awaited book and I am proud to own a copy"

All About Antigua and Barbuda is a travel guide that describes the history and heritage of the twin island nation of Antigua and Barbuda, and highlights some of its most popular sites and attractions.

Review: *This book was very interesting! We used it in our homeschool for this quarter and the children loved it. We are traveling to Antigua later this year and wanted some education on the island. The book covers so many amazing locations while incorporating Antiguan history into the reading!! Can't wait to visit many of the locations we studied in this book!"*

The books listed above are available on Amazon in both paperback and ebook formats

www.ingramcontent.com/pod-product-compliance
Lightning Source LLC
Chambersburg PA
CBHW052057070526
44584CB00017B/2226